From Wild Man to Wise Man

REFLECTIONS ON MALE SPIRITUALITY

Richard Rohr, O.F.M.

With original input from Joseph Martos, Ph.D.
from *The Wild Man's Journey*

ST. ANTHONY MESSENGER PRESS

Cincinnati, Ohio

Scripture passages are the author's own paraphrase.

Cover design by Candle Light Studios
Book design by Phillips Robinette, o.f.m.
Illustration on page 127, executed by Sebastian Dayg in 1511, is from an altarpiece
in the former Cistercian monastery of Heilsbronner Müenster in Germany.

Library of Congress Cataloging-in-Publication Data

Rohr, Richard.
    From wild man to wise man : reflections on male spirituality / Richard Rohr ; with
original input from Joseph Martos from The wild man's journey.
        p. cm.
    Rev. ed. of: The wild man's journey.
    ISBN 0-86716-740-8 (pbk. : alk. paper) 1. Men—Religious life. 2. Men (Christian
theology) 3. Spiritual life—Catholic Church. 4. Men—Psychology. 5. Masculinity—
Religious aspects. I. Martos, Joseph, 1943- II. Rohr, Richard. Wild man's journey. III.
Title.

BX2352.5.R64 2005
248.8'42—dc22
                                        2005017075

ISBN-13 978-0-86716-740-5
ISBN-10 0-86716-740-8

Published by St. Anthony Messenger Press
28 W. Liberty St.
Cincinnati, OH 45202
www.AmericanCatholic.org

Printed in the United States of America

Printed on acid-free paper

05 06 07 08 09 5 4 3 2

A man, yet by these tears a little boy again,
Throwing myself on the sand, confronting the waves,
I, chanter of pains and joys, uniter of here and hereafter,
Taking all hints to use them, but swiftly leaping beyond them,
A reminiscence sing.
—WALT WHITMAN, "Out of the Cradle Endlessly Rocking"

Contents

Editor's Note

You may find it helpful to know the evolution of this book.

In the late 1980s St. Anthony Messenger Press asked Richard Rohr and Joseph Martos to collaborate on a book about male spirituality as a follow-up to their other books published by St. Anthony Messenger Press: *The Great Themes of Scripture: Old Testament* (1987), *The Great Themes of Scripture: New Testament* (1988) and *Why Be Catholic? Understanding Our Experience and Tradition* (1989). At that time, there wasn't much to read about male spirituality.

The Wild Man's Journey: Reflections on Male Spirituality (St. Anthony Messenger Press, 1990) was developed by theologian Joseph Martos and based initially on four talks that Richard gave as a weekend retreat for men only. Women were not invited because the retreat intended to bring up issues of primary concern to men and because portions of the weekend were set aside for small-group sessions in which men could process concerns that they might not raise in the presence of women. The intention was to create an atmosphere in which suppressed doubts and fears, hopes and dreams could safely come to the surface, be listened to and be discussed in frank, man-to-man dialogue.

At Richard's request, Joe Martos incorporated into the book material from Richard's audiocassette programs *A Man's Approach to God* (St. Anthony Messenger Press, 1984) and *The Spirit in a Man* (Credence Cassettes, 1988). The resulting book, *The Wild Man's Journey,* sold very well and was translated into several languages. Richard began to speak about male spirituality across the United States as well as in Europe, most notably in Germany.

Like its author, *The Wild Man's Journey* evolved to reflect the changes and growth in male spirituality, and so Richard revised the book in 1996. The topic of male spirituality continued to appeal and challenge men for over twenty years, and again Richard recognized the need to update and revise his original work.

The book you are holding, *From Wild Man to Wise Man: Reflections on Male Spirituality,* was revised in 2005. For this new work, Richard shortened almost every chapter, changed some chapters significantly and dropped seven chapters from the previous edition. He added three chapters that discuss John the Baptist, Paul and grief. The former afterword has become a very different chapter two, "Is There Such a Thing as Masculine Spirituality?"

An appendix provides a structure for a men's group, based on Richard's work with M.A.L.Es (Men as Learners and Elders), a program of the Center for Action and Contemplation that Richard founded and now directs in Albuquerque, New Mexico.

Richard, in his notes about this latest revision, wrote, "I think *From Wild Man to Wise Man* is a much better book than the previous *The Wild Man's Journey.* The shorter chapters make the book better suited for use by men's small groups. A team of men studied the previous book and gave me much advice on how to make the material more user-friendly."

St. Anthony Messenger Press—and Richard Rohr—invite you to embrace this new *Wild Man.*

Lisa Biedenbach
Editorial Director, Books
St. Anthony Messenger Press
May 2005

ONE

The Wild Man

He's Wild, you know!
　　　　　　　—C.S. LEWIS on God

Perhaps my single greatest disappointment in most of the world's religions is that they succeeded, against all odds, in making most people *afraid* of God! Do you realize how absurd and horrible that is? It pretty much makes it an unsafe and scary universe at the core, where no one is at home and everyone is paranoid. It makes the mystical adventure impossible. It turns religion into a self-serving brokerage business, always picking up the pieces after a kind of "taught and learned helplessness." The result has been massive neuroses, nonstop aggression and a phenomenon unique to the West: atheism. Poor "pagan" India where they told me the first week, "You will not find any atheists in India—except perhaps among those people taught in religious schools."

Anyone who has any authentic inner experience knows that God is only beauty, mercy and total embrace, and nothing but beauty, mercy and total embrace. The Trinitarian nature of God makes that theologically certain.[1] The only people who don't know that are those who have never sought God's face. In my experience there is an almost complete correlation between the degree of emphasis one puts on obligations, moralities, ritual performance and one's lack of any real inner experience. Once you know for yourself, you will be plenty "moral," in fact, even more so, but it all

1

proceeds from a free response, from the Trinitarian flow passing through you. It is a response, not a requirement, an effect of having known love, not a precondition for getting love. *God is always the initiator, always good, always available, and the flow is always free.* Yes, sin is real and common, but it merely means to stop, resist or deny this omnipresent flow of God's love.

Now, believe it or not, we are threatened by such a free God *because it takes away all of our ability to control or engineer the process.* It leaves us powerless, and changes the language from any language of performance or achievement to that of surrender, trust and vulnerability. This is not the preferred language of men! It makes God free and us not. That is the so-called "wildness" of God. We cannot control God by any means whatsoever, *not even by our good behavior,* which tends to be our first and natural instinct. As God said to Moses, "I show compassion on whomever I will, and show pity on whom I please" (Exodus 33:19). That utter and absolute freedom of God is fortunately used totally in our favor, even though we are still afraid of it. It is called providence, forgiveness, free election or mercy by the tradition. But to us, it feels like wildness—*precisely because we cannot control it, manipulate it, direct it, earn it or even lose it.* Anyone into controlling God by his or her actions will feel very useless, impotent and ineffective.

God in the Hebrew Scriptures comes off much wilder than he does in the New Testament (largely because we have civilized and domesticated Jesus from his Jewish roots!). Yahweh, the God of Israel, picks out a guy named Abraham and tells him to pack up his stuff and head out for some place across the desert that he's never seen before. He tells Abraham and his wife, who are both about a hundred years old, that they're going to have a baby—and they do! But then God blows Abraham's mind by ordering him to sacrifice that only son, and this after telling him he will be the father of a great nation! This has nothing to do with order, certitude, clarity, reason, logic, church authority or merit! This is an utterly free God trying to create spiritually free people. I am philosophically and theologically committed to keeping God absolutely free.[2] In general God has not been very free, either with Jews, Christians or Muslims, all of whom call themselves "children of Abraham."

The Israelites, later on, think they've got it made because they're God's chosen people, but God continually undercuts them for not being as compassionate as the God they claim to love. God is not a "company man" and does not appear to be calling for company or tribal values. Yahweh is the God of "all the peoples" and forms his own "rainbow coalition." Yahweh freely chooses his instruments apart from any preconditions of worthiness, sin-lessness, racial purity, orthodoxy, group belonging or lineage. It is almost the theme of themes of the whole Bible. Why? Probably because perfect freedom is the very nature of true love. Without freedom there is no love—only duty, fear and obligation. God does not love us because God has to. God loves us because God wants to. God does not love us because we are good. God loves us because God is good. Why can't we surrender to that? Because it initially feels like a loss of power and importance!

The prophets, too, were a wild bunch. They had to be because they were the spokespeople of a wild God, a God who didn't care much about temples and offerings but who cared a lot about the way people were treated and the opening of the human heart. Read Hosea 6:6, Isaiah 1:11 or Psalm 51:16 if you doubt. We tend to think the prophets were fortune-tellers predicting the Christian future, but they were much more, naming the ever-present illusions and self-deceptions. They were non-clergy with a radical message from a God seeking intimacy, and for all their efforts they largely got persecution and death (see Matthew 23:29–36), down to the last of the prophets, John the Baptist. Nice religion is always threatened by the "glorious freedom of the children of God" (Romans 8:21). Suddenly God is in charge instead of my explanations of things. I love to remind people that the word "nice" is never found in the whole Bible. God is not nice, it seems; God is wild.

If God's people are, in fact, nice, it is because they are first of all wildly free to break the rules of tit for tat and quid pro quo, and love as God loves: "If you love those who love you, so what? Even the pagans do that!" says Jesus (Matthew 5:46–48). That is just first-stage morality, what Jesus calls "the virtue of the scribes and Pharisees"—which is a level of virtue! But John the Baptist, the son of a priest, yet the archetypal wild man, is the perfect patron saint for many men today because of the way that he moved beyond mere nice religion and created his own initiation ritual. Yet Jesus "submitted" to his whole offbeat, unorthodox show, something really quite amazing.[3] The full male journey is a risky journey where you can only trust God and not your own worthiness or rightness. It is a journey into the outer world, into the world of risk, uncertainty and almost certain failure. Find me a male myth, fairy tale or legend that does not follow that cycle. They are always about journeys into new lands and places, they are always in nature (where we are not in charge), and they always lead you back home "to know it for the first time." Yet many men prefer to remain safely in the world of ideas and opinions and roles of esteem and status. Jeremiah capitalized it as "the sanctuary, the sanctuary, the sanctuary! Put no trust in delusive words like these" (7:4). There is almost no energy stored there, until you have once left the sanctuary, and finally know what it really means.

Part of the difficulty, of course, is that in our western culture and even in our religious tradition we have few guides to lead us deeply into the full male journey and almost no mentors who have been there themselves and come back to guide us through. We are longing for believable mentors on every stage of the male journey. (Forgive me, but most of us who are attracted to the clergy role are largely "inner and idea" people and usually not risk takers or very broad in our experience.) Much of my hope in *From Wild Man to Wise Man* is that we can lead men through some new stages of their journey, maybe even to understand their wildness in a way that might be wisdom.

Interestingly enough, our word "mentor" comes from Greek mythology. Mentor was the wise and trusted counselor of Odysseus. When Odysseus went on his long journey, he put Mentor in charge of his son, Telemachus, as his teacher and the guardian of his soul. This illustrates that one's biological father is seldom the initiator of the son. It is always another special man who must guide the boy into manhood, from wildness to wisdom. (Perhaps much of our problem today is that we have so few "god-fathers" and that we expect from our biological fathers far too much!)

In men's work we speak of the uninitiated man as the *puer* (Latin for boy or child). If we have many *puers* today, it is not only because we have little knowledge of the rather universal initiation rites for young men[4] but also because we have so few mentors and guides on those journeys. Much of our work today in M.A.L.Es (Men as Learners and Elders) is trying to raise up a new first generation of men who can pass on the wisdom and create a new tradition of initiation. Part of our problem is that too many men confuse primal initiation (read "conversion" if you will) with being churchy, law abiding and nice. This largely misses the point.

Many bosses, ministers, coaches and teachers tell a young man how to get out of his problems and to be "normal" again. A true mentor or initiator guides a young man *into* his problems and *through* them, which will always feel a bit muddy and messy, but also wet and wild and wise. The mentor will lead a man to The Center, and to his own center, but by circuitous paths, using even his two steps backward to lead him three steps forward. It looks wild, but it is really the wisdom path of God.

Notes

1. Richard Rohr, "The Divine Dance" (Center for Action and Contemplation, Box 12464, Albuquerque, NM 87195, 2004), four CDs on the revolutionary yet largely overlooked implications of the Christian doctrine of God as a Trinity.

2. Mary Beth Ingham, *Scotus for Dunces* (St. Bonaventure, N.Y.: Franciscan Institute, 2003), p. 49ff. Blessed John Duns Scotus (1266–1308), who has influenced my thinking profoundly, was a Franciscan philosopher and theologian. He insisted and taught on the absolute and total freedom of God, to act according to God's own nature. God's love is not determined by the object but by the subject. That freedom was then extended to all creatures, who each must act and live according to their "thisness," as Scotus called it.

3. Richard Rohr, *Soul Brothers: Men in the Bible Speak to Men Today* (Maryknoll, N.Y.: Orbis Books, 2004). Note especially the chapter on John the Baptist, "The First Necessary Freedom," p. 43ff.

4. Richard Rohr, *Adam's Return: The Five Promises of Male Initiation* (New York: Crossroad, 2004). This book is my attempt to communicate the core messages of male initiation and some of its history.

Two

Is There Such a Thing as Masculine Spirituality?

Stillness is what creates love,
Movement is what creates life,
To be still,
Yet still moving—
That is everything!

—DO HYUN CHOE, Japanese Master

Perhaps the term sounds new, strange, even wrong or unnecessary. Why would we bother speaking of a spirituality that is especially masculine or male? Is there anything to be learned here? Don't we all come to God the same way? I am convinced that there are different paths because men and women *pay attention to different things.* Moviemakers know that, book publishers know that, advertisers know that, salespersons know that, almost everybody knows that except the clergy. Fortunately, it is strongly validated in universal sacred stories, legends and myths, which are invariably written for men *or* women, and different patterns are found in the Judeo-Christian Scriptures, too. That will be evident by the end of this book.

First, I want to say that a masculine spirituality is not just for men, although it is men who are most likely going to have to rediscover and exemplify it. Strangely, it is an approach that many women are more in touch with today than men. Women have been

7

encouraged and even forced to work on their inner lives more than men in our culture. They are more open to the whole terrain, for some reason.

In general, women are ahead of men in recognizing their feminist perspective, and also in integrating the *so-called* "feminine" and "masculine" parts of themselves. Their inner journeys and outer scholarship have left many of us men in the dust. Our sisters' pursuit of the feminine voice has made men aware that there must be an authentic masculine somewhere. But what is it? We know instinctively that masculinity cannot be the same as patriarchy.

Quite simply, it is the other side of feminine energy. It is the other pole, the complement, the balance, the counterpoise. I know I am taking a great risk in saying this. Many believe that it is a unisex universe, and all gender distinctions are culturally and artificially created. Even if that were true, although I believe that is too easy closure on the subject, I think both men and women can immensely profit from learning by comparison and contrast, without denying that there are many degrees and stages in between any classic polarities. Think of it as a pedagogical tool, a way of learning.

In the Chinese view of the universe, for example, it is the yang, or masculine principle, that is always the necessary complement to yin, the feminine principle. For the Judeo-Christian tradition, it is half of the image of God: "God created man in his image...male and female he created them" (Genesis 1:27). Sexuality itself is the longing for wholeness between the two. The archetypal pattern is so deep that even many languages have masculine and feminine words.

I am not saying that males are characterized by exclusively masculine energy and that females hold only feminine. In fact, quite the contrary, although there has been a tendency in most cultures to stereotype, classify and hold the sexes in one predictable type of energy and behavior. Unfortunately this tendency has kept us immature, unwhole, compulsive and unready for living a life of love—human or divine.

Saint Paul says, "...there is not male and female; for you are all one in Christ Jesus" (Galatians 3:28). The new humanity that we are pointed toward is not neuter or unisex or even oversexed, all of which make love impossible. In Christ we are whole, one, in union, integrated, wholly holy. That is the final product of the Spirit's work of making all things one. It is the consummate achievement of God in Christ who reconciles all things within himself (Colossians 1:20) and invites us into the ongoing reconciliation of all things (Ephesians 5:20).

As an unmarried male, I can make little sense of my state unless I find some way to awaken and love my own inner feminine soul. Without it, I am merely a self-centered bachelor, a dreamy creator, a dried-up root. A man without his feminine soul is easily described. His personality will move toward the outer world of things, and his head will be his control tower. He will build, explain, use, fix, manipulate, legislate, order and play with whatever he bothers to touch, but he will not really touch it at all—for he does not know the inside of things. He has no subtlety, imagination, ability to harmonize, or live with paradox or mystery. He engineers reality instead of living it.

In fact, he is afraid of real life, and that is why the control tower of reason and pseudo control works overtime. It is the only way he can give himself a sense of security and significance. He is trapped in part of the picture, which is dangerous precisely because he thinks it is the whole picture. "Because you say, 'I see,' you in fact remain blind," as Jesus said (John 9:41). Corporately, this has become the myth of western civilization. It is largely written by men who have controlled the power, the money, the corporations, the church, the military, the morality books. What we call reality, and are almost totally addicted to, is largely a construct of men who have frankly not worked much on their inner lives. They have not gone inside, they have not learned trust, vulnerability, prayer or poetry. They, and the civilization we have inherited from them, are in great part unwhole and even sick. That should not need much defense.

Until males and cooperating females recognize this un-wholeness, this anti-Incarnationalism posing as reality, we have no hope of loving or knowing God. We will, in fact, be threatened by wholeness and replace (as we generally have) any daring Biblical faith with little schemes of salvation. Thomas Merton called them "private holiness projects." Psychologists call them ego agendas. In men's work, we call it "building our tower." Basically, this is a transfer of the business world of win…achieve…prove… succeed…control to the realm of the Spirit. And it just doesn't work. It is the anti-gospel. There *is* a better way.

For starters, a masculine spirituality would emphasize movement over stillness, action over theory, service to the world over religious discussions, speaking the truth over social niceties and doing justice instead of any self-serving "charity." Without a complementary masculine, spirituality becomes overly feminine (which is really a false feminine!) and is characterized by too much inwardness, preoccupation with relationships, a morass of unclarified feeling and religion itself as a security blanket. This prevents a journey to anyplace new, and fosters a constant pro-tecting of the old. It is no-risk religion, just the opposite of Abraham, Moses, Paul and Jesus.

In my humble masculine opinion I believe much of the modern, sophisticated church is swirling in what I will describe as a kind of "neuter" religion. It is one of the main reasons that doers, movers, shakers and change agents have largely given up on church people and church groups. As one very effective woman said to me, "After a while you get tired of the in-house jargon that seems to go nowhere." A neuter spirituality is the trap of those with lots of leisure, luxury and self-serving ideas. They have the option not to do, not to change, not to long and thirst for justice. It can take either a liberal or a conservative form, but in either case, it becomes an inoculation against any deep spiritual journey. That's why I call it "neuter." It generates no real sexual energy or life.

A masculine spirituality would be one that encourages men to take the radical gospel journey from their own unique beginning point, in their own unique style, with their own unique goals—which is what we end up doing anyway, but now with no doubt or apology or need to imitate our sisters or even our fathers, for that matter. That takes immense courage and self-possession. Such a man has life for others and knows it. He does not need to push, intimidate or play the power games common to other men because he possesses his power with surety and calm self-confidence. He is not opinionated or arrogant, but he *knows*. He is not needy of status symbols because he draws his identity from God and from within. He does not need monogrammed briefcases and underwear; his identity is settled and secure. He possesses his soul and does not give it lightly to corporations, armies, nation-states or the acceptable collective thinking. He is beyond red state and blue state thinking.

Male saints are, quite simply, people who are whole. They trust their masculine soul because they have met the good masculine side of God, whom we have called "The Father." The Father taught them about anger, passion, power and clarity. He told them to go all the way through and pay the price for it. He shared with them his own creative seed, his own decisive word, his own illuminating Spirit. They are comfortable knowing, and they are comfortable not knowing. They can care and not care—without guilt or shame. They can act without success because they have named their fear of failure. They do not need to affirm or deny, judge or ignore. But they are free to do all of them with impunity. A saint is invincible.

There are many reasons, I'm sure, why a healthy masculine spirituality has taken so long to emerge. The state needed conformists and unfeeling warriors to go about its business, and "holy Mother Church" seemed to want children more than what Jesus called "bridegrooms," and I would call mystics. But I am convinced there is a more fundamental reason why men and women have failed to love and trust their masculine energy. It is this: The vast majority of people in western civilization suffer from what I will identify in this book as the "father wound." Those who have this father wound have never been touched by their human father. Either he had no time, no freedom or no need, but the result is children who have no masculine energy. They will lack self-confidence and the ability to do, to carry through, to trust themselves—because they were never trusted by him. They fear and sometimes even hate the masculine side of God, for very understandable reasons. But the loss has been incalculable.

If there is one very good reason for God to reveal himself as the Father of Jesus, it is because that is where most people are wounded—unfeeling, unbelieving and unwhole. With Philip the Apostle, we all join in, "Master, show us the Father, and that will be enough for us" (John 14:8). Without facing, feeling and healing this wound, I am sure that most men will continue to live lives of pseudo-masculinity: business and bravado as usual, dishonest power instead of honest powerlessness. And the sons and daughters of the next generation will repeat the sad process all over again.

Today, too many of God's sons are without dignity, self-confidence or true power. They have little inner authority, and pre-dictably over-rely upon outer authority. *They look like the oppressors, but have no doubt they are really the oppressed.* We believed the false promises of the system even more than women and are now trapped at what is supposed to be the top. We need true friendship, male and female; we need our also-feminine-souls; we need fathers and brothers; we need a good and also-masculine-God to find our way back into the human circle. We need ourselves—from the inside. Yet we need to act—on the outside. It is a dance.

The spiritual man in mythology, in literature and in the great world religions has an *excess of life,* he *knows* he has it, makes no apology for it, and finally recognizes that he does not even need to protect or guard it. It is not for him. It is for others. His life is not his own. His life is not about him. It is about God.

THREE

Male and Female God Created Them

The man stood at the door and knocked.
The woman inside said, "Who are you?"
The man outside said, "It's me!"
The door remained closed.
She asked again, "Who are you?"
This time he answered, "It is you!"
And the door was fully opened to him.

In the Bible humanity is created both male and female in order to image God (Genesis 1:27), yet that distinction between man and woman is made only after their original union with one another and with God (Genesis 2:18–23). Thus all healthy spirituality will always have a truly "sexual" character to it, a desire for re-union. Religion is always, in one sense or another, about *making one out of two!* Cheap religion is invariably about maintaining the *two* and keeping things separate and apart. Think about that and see if it is not true.

For countless ages, however, human culture and society have emphasized the differences between men and women rather than their underlying unity. Despite the endless fascination of the sexes for one another, social customs have sharply distinguished maleness from femaleness and sexual morality has been concerned with keeping men and women apart. It is probably why homosexual persons are such a threat to most societies. Our society has taught us to regard the opposite sex with suspicion, and our culture has bred in us a spirit of competition for different forms of power.

Since most cultures have been patriarchal or dominated by men, women are usually viewed, and often are, an oppressed group in society. Men have all the visible power and women are the losers. In my own reflections on the male-female tension, however, I have come to see that both of us are the losers. We are deprived of that healthy wholeness—and, I would even say, holiness—which comes from integrating both the masculine and the feminine in our lives as men or women. I would like to suggest that men even suffer greater deprivation than women. As one of Jesus' most popular one-liners says very clearly, "the last will be first and the first last." It is not good to be on the "top."

Women can often compensate for the role in which they have been cast by finding power in indirect ways, such as subtly learning to manipulate and cajole for their needs. It made them much more creative in the ways of power. In other words, they learned the dance between power and powerlessness in ways that men never did. We men have not had a similar avenue open to us. Female behavior was so strictly taboo that men have been blocked from recognizing and developing the feminine dimension within themselves. Again, women got to develop both parts and got what I believe is a significant head start in understanding the very nature of spirituality, particularly Christian spirituality.

In recent years theologians in the Third World have made it very clear that much of the gospel proclaimed by Jesus and lived by the early church was concerned with liberation *in this world.* "As now, so later!" The "good news" (which is the root meaning of the word *gospel*) is that people can be freed from the oppression, illusion and death that binds them. Heaven is only its continuation. The first people to accept and respond to the gospel message of liberation were, of course, the poor and the powerless. They were blessed because they knew that they were unwhole and in need of healing/*salus*/salvation (Matthew 5:3–12).

Much of Jesus' teaching, however, was directed not at the poor but at the rich; not at the weak but at the powerful. Jesus evidently saw the oppressors (often typified in the first three Gospels as "the scribes and the Pharisees") with an even greater need because they were trapped by their own self-sufficiency (Matthew 23:13–39). We know it is still true today. The rich are deprived by their own wealth, the powerful are victimized by their own positions, the oppressors are oppressed by their own domination. They hardly ever see it that way, but try to think of a great spiritual teacher in any of the world religions who does not say such things.

If this is the case, then women have nothing to gain by turning the situation upside down. Some feminists seem to believe that if the male-female roles could be reversed, women would be liberated from oppression in our patriarchal society and that gender affirmative action will resolve all of our problems. If the roles are simply reversed, however, women would become just as trapped as men now are, but in a matriarchal or woman-dominated system.

The liberating gospel of Jesus is that salvation is found not in domination but in partnership, not in power-wielding but in power-sharing. The poor are not saved by robbing the rich. The weak are not saved by conquering the strong. The oppressed are not saved by making the masters their slaves. Turning the tables simply perpetuates the sinful human situation that Jesus was engaged in redeeming.

The spiritually whole person integrates within himself or herself both the masculine and the feminine dimensions of the human spirit. She or he is androgynous in the best sense of that term, which is derived from the two Greek words meaning "man" and "woman."[1] It is very fascinating that some tribes and civilizations actually considered the man-woman to actually be the *shaman*, the wise man, the spiritual seer. They were the image of Divine wholeness. Androgyny is the ability to be masculine in a womanly way and to be feminine in a manly way, if I can dare to say it that way. It probably takes the work of a lifetime to get there, which is the beauty we often see in older men and women. The young man is all "male," and the young girl is all "sugar and spice and everything nice." If you read classic legends and myths, note how you invariably meet the strong, old woman and the kind, old man by the end of the story. That is the goal.

Note

1.   For more on androgyny, read *The Invisible Partners*, by John A. Sandford (Paulist Press, 1980).

FOUR

The Addictive System

In a world of fugitives,
the person taking the opposite direction will appear to
run away.

—T.S. Eliot, *The Family Reunion*[1]

Anne Wilson Schaef is a psychologist who in recent years has written a number of books about addiction and codependence, caused not only by drugs but also by the way people think and behave in modern society.[2] When she first began writing about the social system that we in Europe and North America live and work in, she labeled it the white male system because these cultures are dominated by white males. Afterward, however, she came to the realization that many women have also bought into this system and that they defend it just as strenuously as most men do, as do some nonwhites. She also saw that this is but one of a number of systems that people in our society are addicted to, so she analyzed much of what is going on in the United States today in terms of its being an addictive society. That is probably a better word.

Schaef believes, and strongly validates, that the overwhelming majority of men in our society are addicted to ways of thinking, feeling and acting that systematically entrap them without their realizing it, in much the same way that alcohol, nicotine or other drug addictions subtly but securely ensnare their victims. They believe they are the lords of the social reality that they define, but actually they are imprisoned in it. The four walls of their prison cell are what Schaef calls four myths—overarching beliefs that define the mental world in which most men live.

The first myth is that *the white male system is the only system there is.* Men who are caught up in this world know no other way of looking at reality. They are addicted to a one-dimensional view of the world, and this defines reality for them. There is no other game in town but the game of power, status and wealth. It is the game that is played in the boardrooms of corporate America, on the stock and commodity exchanges, on the playing fields of professional sports, in local and national governments, in the ranks of factory and office workers and in the neighborhoods of suburbia. The list could be endlessly expanded because the myth embraces, in one way or another, everything in our lives. It is the way we all live. To one extent or another, we are all addicted to this system, men and women, and to the reality it defines for us.

The second myth is that *the white male system is innately superior.* Other people may have other ways of thinking, feeling and behaving, but they are out of touch with what we take for granted as reality, or even more cynically, "the bottom line." Our attitudes and actions are at best quaint and amusing, and at worst wrong and threatening. From this position of superiority, those in the system can stand in judgment of those outside it. Women can be labeled as weak, blacks as incompetent, Chicanos as lazy, Russians as untrustworthy, the poor as unproductive, the uneducated as ignorant, the unborn as disposable. The list is as long as the list of white male prejudices. For the system defines what is right and good and true. It is just the corporate shape of the inherent narcissism that characterizes all uninitiated people.[3]

The third myth is that *the white male system knows and understands everything.* There is nothing that falls outside its purview or, if it does, it is unimportant. The system and those who dominate the system understand what is best for everybody and what is best for the world. They know what God wants, and they understand how God wants people to live. They can, therefore, legislate economy, policy and even morality. The system and those who are addicted to it have no doubts about the way things are and the way things ought to be. In my opinion, this arrogance has actually taken religious form in much of western Christianity, and I say that after thirty-five happy years as a Catholic priest.

The fourth myth is the belief that *it is possible for us to be totally logical, rational and objective.* Everything that is worth knowing is objectifiable and quantifiable. It can be counted as part of the gross national product, it can be measured and weighed in the balance of political power, it can be observed and analyzed by some science or another, or it can be legislated or covered under some law or other. If there is something that cannot be known through the technology of the system, it is irrelevant, and it can be disregarded. Feelings, values, hopes, ideals, rights and other intangibles only count when they can be quantified and measured.

Although the first three myths reveal how partial and incomplete the white male system really is, the fourth myth shows why it is so addictive. Like the alcoholic who engages in what Alcoholics Anonymous calls "stinkin' thinkin'," people caught up in this system engage in very limited thinking and perceiving. It is all-or-nothing thinking, dualistic thinking or you are either with me or you are against me thinking. There is not much hope of creating a united anything. Peoples' addiction to their own system blinds them to anything and everything that falls outside that system. *What they see and feel is only what feeds their addiction or what threatens it.* To themselves they seem logical, even when they are being incoherent. To themselves they seem reasonable, even when they are being irrational. To themselves they seem moral, even when they are doing things that are destroying themselves and others. It is why many alcoholics are unkindly called "dry drunks" even after they stop drinking. The thinking patterns are still either/or and do not read reality very well.

Anne Wilson Schaef further suggests that these four myths are capped by yet another myth that addicts all support, much as the four walls of a cell support the ceiling that encapsulates the prisoner within it. Like the ceiling, no one pays much attention to it, but it is there. It is the de facto belief that *it is therefore possible for us to be God.* This is, of course, the very temptation of the snake in the garden (Genesis 3:5). Most white males would, of course, deny that this is a part of their belief system, but that is because they do not look up to see what their beliefs ultimately lead to. If God is the one superior being who exists, who defines reality and who knows everything, then by creating and maintaining the addictive system white males are wittingly or unwittingly playing God.

I caught a glimpse of this when Bob Woodward wrote a book in which he questioned former CIA director William Casey.[4] Casey's wife called any questioning of her husband "blasphemy"! Now as a good Irish Catholic she should know that blasphemy is a word to describe an offense against God. How strange that she would consciously or unconsciously equate God and the CIA, or American security needs with something that God never promised us nor Jesus ever praised. Yet we often think that way as a whole nation and never see the contradiction. Many groups do.

What is truly blasphemous is the replacement of God with the white male system and the way that the system arrogates the attributes of God to itself. Call it patriotism, call it national self-interest, call it company loyalty or call it faithfulness to your church; the demand for unquestioning allegiance and blind obedience is the same demand that a drug makes on an addict. If people are to develop any deep spirituality today, and especially if men are to develop spiritually, they need to be liberated from self-serving worldviews. Male mythologies usually represented this as the necessary killing of the dragon. We just call it conversion, *metanoia* (new mind), repentance, transformation or initiation. Pick your preferred word, but every mature religion insists that it *must* happen, or we will not be situated correctly inside of the universe.

Notes

1. T.S. Eliot, *The Family Reunion* (New York: Harcourt, Brace Jovanovich Publishers, 1939), p. 110.

2. Her works include *Women's Reality: An Emerging Female System in a White Male Society* (San Francisco: Harper & Row, 1986), *When Society Becomes an Addict* (San Francisco: Harper & Row, 1987) and *The Addictive Organization: Why We Overwork, Cover Up, Pick Up the Pieces, Please the Boss and Perpetuate Sick Organizations,* coauthored with Diane Fassell (San Francisco: Harper & Row, 1988).

3. Rohr, *Adam's Return.* This is my most complete attempt to analyze what initiation was trying to do for men and culture.

4. Bob Woodward, *Veil: The Secret Wars of the CIA 1981-1987* (New York: Simon and Schuster, 1987).

FIVE

Men's Liberation

*There are two ways of being a prophet. One is to tell
the enslaved that they can be free. It is the difficult
path of Moses. The second is to tell those who think
they are free that they are in fact enslaved. This is the
even more difficult path of Jesus.*

—RICHARD ROHR

My very first assignment as a deacon was with the Acoma
Native American tribe in New Mexico. Before I drove to visit them,
the other Franciscans tried to prepare me for a culture shock by
telling me how different these people are. They said that the
Acomas are a matriarchal society in which the women are the real
leaders of the tribe. It is the women who are strong, who make the
decisions and who tell the men what to do. If I wanted to work with
these people, I was advised, I would have to learn to work with
the women.

Thus forewarned, I spent my initial time at the reservation just
observing and listening, trying to learn the social patterns that
prevailed among them. After a few weeks, however, it dawned on
me that there wasn't much difference between these people and
the folks back home. The only thing different was that the Acoma
were honest about the way their society works. The women have

the real power and everyone admits it, whereas in white society everyone pretends that men are in charge and women are helpless. We men think we call the shots, but many of the day-to-day decisions that actually control our lives are made by women. Men's power is largely economic, political and physical, and Jesus would question whether that is power at all, even though there are clear justice issues involved there, too.

An anecdote I read somewhere conveys this idea humorously but pointedly. When asked who makes the decisions in his family, a man replied that his wife makes all the little decisions and she lets him make all the big decisions. Pressed to clarify what he meant by that, he explained, "My wife decides what neighborhood we should live in, what schools are best for the children, how to budget our money, where we should go on vacation, who we socialize with, and things like that. But I decide the big issues, like whether we should trust the Russians, whether the government is doing a good job, and what we should do about the economy." The story is both funny and sad because the man has obviously been hoodwinked into believing that those are the "big" decisions in his daily life.

Even on the job, most men do not have much power. If they are blue-collar workers, they do what they are told to do, which is usually the same thing over and over again every day. If they are supervisors or managers, there is always some boss higher up telling them what to do and what not to do. If they are salespeople, they are always trying to please their customers. Even if they are executives, most of their so-called decisions are determined by company protocols and policies, by boards of directors and by market forces beyond their control. Most men are paid for doing what someone else wants done. They do not really control their own lives. No wonder so many men have become passive, and no wonder that so many men seem to be angry.

This lack of control is why entertainment and vacation are so important for most men. The stresses of always meeting someone else's deadlines, of living up to someone else's expectations and of knowing that another man is ready to step into his job if he performs poorly make it necessary to periodically get out of the rat race and forget how tense he is. So he can't really decide not to watch television or not to go out on the weekend or not to take a vacation because he really needs those escapes from his daily grind. Work is not re-creative, so he seeks recreation. Our culture presents men with the illusion of making decisions, but it effectively castrates them from charting actual new directions beyond and outside of the rat race. Men hardly ever have a chance to make decisions that make a real difference in their own lives or in the world around them, except in a minor diversionary way. They have to play the game or they won't be rewarded.

Another indication of this is how few people in America bother to vote. On the surface, we pride ourselves on our democracy, but less than half the eligible voters turn out for national elections and even fewer than that bother to vote in local elections. The president of the United States, for instance, is regularly elected by only about a quarter of the adults in our country. When questioned by pollsters, many Americans say they do not vote because they feel powerless to change the system or because they see no real difference between the candidates. No matter who wins, they say, the real decisions in the government will be controlled by powerful lobbies, business interests and multinational corporations that are more powerful than most governments. They do not bother to write Congress or to join citizens' action groups for essentially the same reasons.

The addictive system, therefore, offers the illusion of power and freedom while holding back any real decision-making power. This is also why it must offer illusions of success—promotions, paychecks and other symbols of prestige—to men who subconsciously know that moving to another niche in the maze is no escape from the totally controlling game they are forced to play. A larger desk, a private office, a bigger house, a newer car, a more expensive vacation—such are the essentially empty rewards men receive for surrendering their freedom and draining their masculine energy in the service of business as usual.

Men are taught the rules of the system quite early in their lives. When I was teaching in Roger Bacon High School in Cincinnati in 1970 and 1971, most of the boys were what you would call normal. They were smart, average looking, healthy and on some kind of fast track. And yet the overwhelming majority of them felt bad about themselves. If they couldn't be elected to the student senate, if they didn't look like movie stars, if they couldn't make the football team, they felt like they were nothing. You'd hope that a Franciscan high school would offer them a more Christian outlook on life, but it operated largely on the same set of values that the rest of the world works on. Catholic education, like all education in our culture, teaches the motivations and rewards of the white male system in which the individual is always blamed for failure, never the system itself.[1]

Part of our oppression as men, of course, is that we are taught to oppress others who have less status than we do. It creates a pecking order and a sense of superiority. We especially oppress racial minorities, homosexuals, the poor and women. Psychologically we have to do this in order to have some feeling of superiority in the absence of any real accomplishments. When we are prevented from making any actual difference in the world, we create illusions of difference in order to have any self-esteem at all. For some reason, the ego creates itself by comparison and competition. I don't really have to do anything that great myself; I just have to know that I am *better, higher, stronger, smarter* than the other guy. This is a strange and finally self-defeating model for male growth. It is called the scapegoat mechanism. I am good just because someone else is bad.

Men's liberation is, therefore, even more difficult than women's liberation. Women know that they are oppressed, and that in itself is the beginning of liberation. Women know the games men play, whereas we men do not even recognize the system as a set of games. Even when we do recognize it, we believe that's simply the way the world is, the way life has to be. But it is not the way life has to be. There is a way out. *You just stop believing it!* Look elsewhere for your payoffs and energy. In biblical language it is called *salvation:* being saved from the world and its false promises, being saved from ourselves—much more than being saved from "hell." Of course, you will never have the ability or courage to stop believing the illusion, until you have something *more* and *better* to take its place. That's where a truly loving God comes in. God gives the healthy soul an utterly new frame of reference *outside* this system.

I often feel, as Thomas Merton said, like a conductor on a train that he knows is heading toward a certain cliff. He runs up and down the aisles telling the people to get off before it is too late, and they only gawk in wonder at his obvious incoherence and hysteria. You cannot liberate anybody until they are convinced they need liberation. In poorer cultures this is somewhat easy. Here, in our culture, we have just enough middle-class comfort and limited freedom to avoid the question for an awfully long time—sometimes for all our lives. No wonder Jesus made what is called his most ignored statement, and is certainly one of the most offensive and shocking: "It is harder for a rich man to know what I am talking about, than for a camel to pass through the eye of a needle" (see Matthew 19:24; Mark 10:25; Luke 18:25). Why don't popes and priests ever make infallible and doctrinal statements about that? Maybe because we are rich men ourselves, enjoying too much the fruits of the system that we are supposed to call into question.

Note

1. Richard Rohr, "The Spiral of Violence: The World, the Flesh, and the Devil," a recorded talk given in Albuquerque in 2005 (Center for Action and Contemplation, Box 12464, Albuquerque, NM 87195).

Six

Male Initiation

The heroes of all time have gone before us; the labyrinth is thoroughly known; we have only to follow the thread of the hero path. And where we had thought to find an abomination, we shall find a god; where we had thought to travel outward, we shall come to the center of our own existence; and where we had thought to be alone, we shall be with all the world.

—JOSEPH CAMPBELL

In almost all cultures men are not born; they are made. Much more than for women, cultures have traditionally demanded initiation rites specifically for the boys. It is almost as if the biological experiences of menstruation and childbirth are enough wisdom lessons for women, but invariably men must be tried, limited, challenged, punished, hazed, circumcised, isolated, starved, stripped and goaded into maturity. The pattern is nearly universal, and the only real exceptions are the recent secular West. Boy scouts, confirmation classes, Lions clubs and Elks clubs have tried to substitute, but with little spiritual effect.

Historically, the program was clear. The boy had to be separated from protective feminine energy, led into ritual space where newness and maleness could be experienced as holy; the boy had to be ritually wounded and tested, and there experience

31

bonding with other men and loyalty to tribal values, and then have something to give back. The pattern is so widely documented that one is amazed that we have let go of it so easily. The contemporary experience of gangs, gender identity confusion, romanticization of war, aimless violence and homophobia will all grow unchecked, I predict, until boys are again mentored and formally taught by wise elders. Historically, it was much of the meaning of the medicine man, the priest and the shaman. Now boys look to coaches, drill sergeants and fundamentalist preachers for what the church no longer gives them. In fact, they even resent it from clergymen, probably because we too long gave them stones instead of bread, moral minimals instead of courageous journeys, holy days of obligation instead of risky vision quests.

Male initiation always has to do with hardness, limit situations, difficulty, struggle and usually a respectful confrontation with the nonrational, the unconscious or, if you will, the wild. *It prepares the young man to deal with life in other ways than logic, managing, controlling and problem solving.* Frankly, it prepares him for the confrontation with Spirit.

Because we have no such training today, the modern male is not only trapped inside his comfort zone, but he is also trapped inside of his small psyche and what he thinks is reason. This is the myth of modernism, which has permeated the last few hundred years in the West. It is a myth just as surely as was the myth of Zeus or the myth of Quetzalcoatl or the myth of Adam and Eve. Because our men have not been initiated into the sacred, they think their smaller myth is actually objective truth and universal order. They are so trapped inside of the myth of modernism ("modernism" = philosophy of progress + left brain reason as adequate truth + autonomy and development of the individual) that we are less and less capable of encountering any true Transcendent Reality. We just collapsed into the cynicism of "postmodernism" somewhere around 1968, at least in America. When logic and order did not produce "order", we just gave up on it entirely. It produced a shapeless society and psyche. Atheism and agnosticism were unthinkable until the modern and postmodern period.

In classic "salvation stories" and mythic journeys men typically move through several levels of consciousness: from (1) simple to (2) complex to (3) enlightened. There are much finer distinctions within these, but for our purposes here, these three will suffice. It matches the advice of the Zen master who says to start with the common-sense answer, then think, study, wait, struggle and search as if it all depended on you, which is complex consciousness where many people stay, but it should lead you back to the simple common-sense answer, but in a whole new way that is not common sense at all. Some call it enlightenment.

The *puer,* or uninitiated male, starts in simple consciousness. Everything is wondrous and true, black and white, filled with mystery and meaning right beneath the surface. We are true believers until about age seven or eight, although some folks are able to retain simple consciousness much longer. It is an innocence ("un-woundedness") that many people in protected families and uncomplicated societies enjoy for much of their lives. It is naïve, and perhaps dangerous to stay there too long, but is characterized by a rich inner life of stories, fantasy and religious meanings that allow people to walk through great difficulty unscathed. They just go inside and find their transcendent purpose, and all injustices, contradictions and sufferings can be dealt with. It is the divine therapy that has carried many people through life since the beginning of time. It is quite simply called belief or faith. It works like nothing else. It is Adam and Eve in the garden, at one with themselves, the animals, creation and God.

But we have to leave the garden to write the rest of the Bible. We invariably "eat of the tree of the knowledge of good and evil" and move into complex consciousness. We get educated, start thinking, managing and trying to control the data. We become a mass of contradictions and opinions, and helpful denials and assertions. We know the answer is out there somewhere, and we keep listening for answers, reading books and hunkering down with pro tem certitudes until the next anxiety attack.

This is most of the journey, where we necessarily live amidst Scylla and Charybdis, the Minotaur and the Sirens. It is the Israelites wandering in circles for forty years in the desert. It is the modern, educated liberal thinker looking for final truth in feelings, explanations, the next book and political correctness. In complex consciousness we know too much to go back to the wonder and peace of the childhood garden, symbolized by the cherubim with flaming swords that guard the return to the tree of life (see Genesis 3:24).

For many, however, the fascinations of complex consciousness keep them inside it forever. It is the angst and the burden of modern men. They keep trying to figure it out with their small mind and heart. Somehow its logic and parameters must eventually fail them. Most western people are trapped in complex consciousness and keep returning to the same wells for water: the wells of reason, order, control and power. It is good, necessary and predictable. We have to go through it. I know I did. There is no nonstop flight, unfortunately, to enlightenment or salvation. This is the illusion of fundamentalism, in all its forms. We never have to leave a kind of garden. But the trouble is that this is not yet true transformation or salvation! You can't be saved until you have fallen, and they will not allow themselves to experience the fall. It is the classic mistake of the so-called "Pharisee," who always remains "right."

Without the painful second stage there is no desire, no spaciousness, no real understanding of the gift. Normally the hero never passes through to enlightenment until he has sustained a number of wounds, disappointments and paradoxes. It is the struggle with darkness and grief that educates the male soul.

Physically that darkness is experienced as pain and handicap, like the wounded hip of Jacob (Genesis 32:26). Intellectually the darkness and absurdity of things is faced through riddles and koans[1] and dilemmas, like the question of the Sphinx, the Fisher King, or the non-answers of the Zen master. I am convinced that much of Jesus' Sermon on the Mount is the same, but the western church has little patience with his paradoxical wisdom, which is from the enlightened third stage. As a churchman myself, I am convinced that many church thinking and leaders are still in complex consciousness, although some neo-conservatives fearfully remain in stage one and call it holiness.

If we are willing to be led, and our ego can sustain some suffering, we are all led toward "salvation." The hero cannot really intend, choose or even fully decide for enlightenment. He does not know what it is yet! All he can do is be *ready* for it! All of life is really about readying, attuning, awakening. Note how many of Jesus' parables and teachings are about being ready and awake. The easiest substitute, of course, is religion. It substitutes answers and too-easy certitude about past and future for *simple present awareness.* Strange as it seems, institutional religion commonly avoids true enlightenment. It feels too much like dying in its early stages, and most people are not well trained in dying. Initiation is *always* training in dying.[2]

Enlightenment is not so much knowing as unknowing; it is not so much learning as unlearning. It is a second and chosen naïveté, without forgetting all the contradictions and complexity in between. It is more surrendering than concluding, more trusting than fixing and all gratuitous grace, for which you can only give thanks. You cannot get yourself enlightened by any known program, ritual or moral practice. This drives the religionists crazy, but as Jesus said, the Spirit blows wherever it pleases (see John 3:8). All you can do is stay on the journey, listen to its lessons, both agony and ecstasy, and ask for that most rare and crucial of gifts:

true openness, which Jesus called trust or faith. All we can really do is to keep our ego out of the way (usually symbolized by the killing of the dragon in mythology) and ask that we will recognize the secret doorway that God opens out of complex consciousness. That door is usually some form of suffering—physical, relational, emotional, intellectual, structural—for almost all of the enlightened and saved people I have ever met.

Initiation always taught the young men to die before he died, and then he would begin to live. That is a constant truth taught by Jesus, the initial ritual of baptism, the Jewish prophets, Mohammed, the mystics, many of the poor and handicapped, and even by survivors of near death experiences. They all seem to agree on the one thing we all avoid—dying. Apparently it is the best and clearest way to put everything in proper order and alignment. As my father, Saint Francis, put it, "If you have once faced the great death, the second death can do you no harm."

Notes

1. A paradox to be meditated upon that is used to train Zen Buddhist monks to abandon ultimate dependence on reason and to force them into gaining sudden intuitive enlightenment (*Webster's Ninth New Collegiate Dictionary*, 1985).

2. Rohr, *Adam's Return*, p. 92ff and passim.

SEVEN

Separation—Encounter —Return

Whom does the Grail serve?
—Parsifal's crucial question after completing the quest for the grail

The journey toward wisdom finds amazingly uniform patterns in universal mythologies. The hero might have a thousand paths to walk, but there seem to be classic and constant patterns beneath his meanderings. Barry Lopez mirrors my own belief when he says that the truth is best found by looking for a discernible pattern.[1] It is *no* surprise that *the* essential mystery of faith for Christians is not a credal statement as much as a Christ-revealed, but also discernible *pattern.* We call it the *paschal mystery.* It is not so much something you *believe,* as something you learn to do. The mythic and liturgical acclamation is lovely: *Christ has died, Christ is risen and Christ will come again.* Life will be death, failure and absurdity, which can lead to renewal, joy and beauty. This pattern is *inevitable, universal and transformative.* It is almost the story line of every good novel you have ever read. Jesus for Christians is the cosmic and classic mythmaker who reveals and lives this pattern for us and tells us we can trust it. Of course, if we have eyes, the pattern is everywhere, but we just don't want to surrender to it. We need a model and guide.

It is rather common to speak of two births that are necessary to come to enlightenment. The first is natural and biological; the second we must be initiated into and choose. It is not certain that it will happen. Thus great spiritual teachers invariably speak of the necessity of conversion, search and surrender. Before we are "born again" we basically do not understand. We are either innocent, cynical or trapped in passing images. The East calls it blindness, illusion or aimless desire; the Christian West tends to call this once-born state "sin." Sin is much more a state of consciousness (or unconsciousness!) than it is individual immoral actions. Jesus came to take away the "sin" (singular) of the world (see John 1:30). Without the spiritual journey, we have the strange phenomenon of people who supposedly avoid "sins" but are still in the state of sin! They don't cuss, drink or run around, but do so from a totally unenlightened consciousness of fear, disguised self-interest, social convention or even hatred of others who do such things. Let's look at some of the normal patterns of the classic spiritual journey.

Out of a formless, uninitiated life there somehow comes *a call.* Probably it takes the form of longing, loneliness, desire, the knowledge that there must be *more,* a falling apart of the game that once sustained you. The hero is somehow directed beyond his private self on a search toward some transcendent or larger goal. This call can come from within or from without, but the would-be hero is enticed by Otherness, by Mystery, what some would call the Holy. This is the first invitation to rebirth. At this point our yes can take many forms, but eventually there must be a clear trusting and a clear "yes." Many are unfortunately hesitant at this stage. There is no one to tell them what this holy longing means, where it comes from and where it is leading—and that it is God.

The journey continues often with *a protective figure.* Invariably, there is a friend, a "god father," a biography, a saint, a mythical image which aids, encourages and gives strength and direction to the would-be hero. The journey never happens alone. There is always a wise elder, a guardian angel, a patron saint, a spirit guide, a wise teacher who somehow sends us in one crucial direction and warns of the dangers and obstacles that will be encountered along the way. Somehow that guide makes you aware, like Jack Palance in *City Slickers,* of the importance of "one thing." When you come to the "one thing important," as Jesus said to Martha, you move almost instantly from profane space to sacred space.[2] There are always many demons and dragons to be faced, but invariably there is one overriding teacher or guide, whether that be Jesus, Buddha or Krishna. Without that protective figure we lack both courage and focus. Although the negative side has many faces and forms, the positive journey is usually presented as *clear, simple and beautiful*—although still mysterious. Actually, you need to fall in love with your model and guide. You cannot usually have "many gods before you," or your ego will remain the god who picks and chooses which god to obey today. This was why the biblical prophets were always trying to get the Jews to "love only Yahweh" and no other god. It is good psychology, if nothing else.

Next the *threshold experience* normally happens when one's own system of logic, meaning, success and truth break down. As Carl Jung said, a true encounter with the numinous is *always* an annihilation for the ego! It's when Perseus confronts the serpented head of Medusa; it's when Jesus feels betrayed by Peter, Judas, the crowds and finally his own Father; it's when the modern man faces his shadow head on by failure, imprisonment or accusation. For the man to be born, the boy must die. The difficulty with an affluent culture like our own is that "infantile grandiosity" can be maintained well into late life by money, meddling or moving away. Quite simply, there is no room for God within us as long as we are filled with our false selves.[3] As Jesus said, "unless the grain of wheat dies, it remains just a grain of wheat" (see John 12:24). That phrase, by the way, is a classic initiation phrase used in the mystery religions of Asia Minor.

As the cocoon of the false self ("sin") is gradually let go, the true self stands revealed. The true self knows who it is, what it must do and, most excitingly, has the energy to do it—no matter what the price. This is *the task* itself, the sense of vocation, the sense of goal, purpose and challenge that guides every hero's life. Quite simply, a hero is one who gives his life to something bigger than himself. He goes for something and is not just along for the ride, but that something must be larger than his own life. We have grown *very* cynical about the possibility of true heroes. Feathering *your* own nest has become so acceptable that we largely substitute celebrities for heroes. Now you are a "hero" if you make a million dollars, and a fool if you give it away. To turn around the classic hero's journey in favor of self-interest puts us at odds with almost all known literature, legend and oral tradition. It certainly puts us at odds with Jesus, Buddha, Abraham and the saints. When a man cannot do greatness in some real sense, his life has no universal significance or transcendent meaning. He is disconnected from the "love that moves the sun and the other stars," as Dante said. In that sense, his life is a disaster, literally "disconnected from the stars."

But there is one more subtle but crucial step. If you read spiritual stories closely, you will see that there is always *a task within the task,* a struggle alongside the struggle. It is not enough to kill the dragon, save the maiden or even die on the cross. *The real hero's task is to keep love, to find humor, to maintain freedom, to discover joy, to expand vision in the process of killing dragons!* There is no room for pettiness or petulance or self-pity, or one is not, by definition, a hero. The sour saint is no saint at all. Our real demons are interior, quiet and disguised and often show themselves as the "noonday devil," which is that pride, negativity or self-absorption that reveals itself in midlife and spoils the seeming good fruit of early accomplishments. Without spiritual disciplines and regular repentance, far too many of us win many battles but finally lose the war. How utterly sad it has been in my work to meet retired, bitter bishops; sad but "successful" priests; and angry old widowers blaming the world for their loneliness. They had no Sancho Panza to accompany them, it seems, as they tilted at life's windmills. They did the task, but not the real task.

The final stages of "the monomyth of the hero," as Joseph Campbell calls it,[4] are the issues of *return*. The hero typically receives some kind of *gift* or bonus at the end of his quest. Don Quixote is forever searching for the "bread that is better than wheat." Prometheus receives fire, Solomon receives wisdom, Jason receives the golden fleece and Jesus hands over the Spirit. Often the hero receives the eternal feminine in the person of a fair maiden or queen or princess. The holy marriage is completed when they become one and live happily ever after. The kingdom is now healthy and fertile because the masculine and the feminine have become one new reality. But the important thing is that the gift is given over *for others*. The grail is not for power, prestige or private possession. It is always for the sake of the community, for the common good. I wonder if we even understand this stage anymore. Far too often our concern seems to be developing our retirement account, self-serving politics and developing our personal image. No civilization has ever survived unless the elders saw it their duty to pass on gifts of Spirit to the young ones. Is it that we are selfish, or is it that we ourselves have never found the gift ourselves? I suspect it is largely the latter. I don't think most people are terribly selfish. They just don't *know*.

There are no loners among the great heroes. There are no self-made men who clean up the town and ride off into the sunset. It is always obvious in the stories that many characters, advisors and circumstances have formed them by the end—usually in spite of themselves. What the pagan mythologies would have seen as fate or destiny, Christian stories would see as grace or Providence. But in either case the hero is formed and created by his times and his struggles and, most of all, by his enemies. He never creates himself. He is created and almost in spite of himself. He has tragic flaws but learns to use them—or let God use them. In the final paragraphs of the story, the hero invariably *returns home,* back to his community. He rejoins the folk with his transforming gift. Odysseus must return to Ithaca, the saints must help us here on earth, Jesus says his disciples will meet him not in imperial Jerusalem but on the humble roads of hometown Galilee. Finally, the hero is a hero precisely because he knows how to go back home.

Enlightened consciousness, looked at externally, looks amazingly like simple consciousness. Second naïveté can be confused with first innocence by the uninitiated. The sayings of wise and wild men look harmless and irrelevant to those trapped in the complex middle. True wisdom looks amazingly like naïve, silly and even dangerous simplicity—although we would never say it in polite company. The Sermon on the Mount has been deemed poetic nonsense by 95 percent of the Christian establishment for two thousand years. And that, in a word, is why true spiritual teachers like Jesus are always marginalized, dismissed, killed, or worst of all, worshipped. Then we can admire them at a safe distance, like a pious icon, but cleverly ignore both their message and their actual journey.

There is no alternative, no other way to understand, than to go on the whole journey ourselves.

Notes

1. Barry Lopez, *Crossing Open Ground* (New York: Charles Scribner's Sons, 1988), p. 69.

2. Mircea Eliade, *The Sacred and the Profane: The Nature of Religion* (New York: Harcourt, 1957).

3. Richard Rohr, "True Self/False Self," a professionally recorded conference on CD (Center for Action and Contemplation, Box 12464, Albuquerque, NM 87195).

4. Joseph Campbell, *The Hero with a Thousand Faces* (Princeton: Bollingen, 1949), p. 30ff.

EIGHT

John the Baptizer as a Classic Initiator

He will be filled with the Holy Spirit and he will bring back many of the sons of Israel...and he will turn the hearts of their fathers toward them.

—LUKE 1:17

There is no way you can see John the Baptist as a plaster or "pretty" saint. He was inaugurating a new expectation inside of his own tradition, a dangerous iconoclast in his time. John saw *religion as a transformation of the self and society, instead of religion as merely a belonging system.* This is exactly why he was hated by his own belonging system. It was not popular thought then, nor is it now. He ended up being beheaded. Symbolically, we could say his "thoughts" needed to be cut off, destroyed and stopped. It is actually quite amazing that he even makes it into the pantheon of Christian saints, since he fulfills few of its orthodox requirements, but fortunately the Scriptures give us no choice—"no man born of woman is greater than John the Baptist"! (see Matthew 11:11; Luke 7:28).

All four Gospel narratives give John the Baptist a lot of press, even though his watch is short, his message appears to be different from that of Jesus, and in some ways he is not that attractive a figure. I am convinced that what the texts are really saying is that he was offering a new "transformation system" that was outside of the priestly and temple system. He was presenting a new "initiating" message and ritual that was clearly a critique of the old, so much so that "the Pharisees and lawyers" would not accept it (Luke 7:30). Nor do we, if we would be honest.

Yet *Jesus did accept it, both publicly and personally.* This places Jesus in an outsider position from the beginning, a point that has often been overlooked. Jesus' acceptance of a riverfront initiation from John put him in a critical stance toward temple religion. That is John's clear role in the Gospel text, and it cannot be sentimentalized away. John was utterly faithful to Torah, Prophets and Wisdom, which led him to critique how it was really playing out. His radical traditionalism made him popular with the crowds, but unpopular with the religious establishment. The intuitive sense of the ordinary people *(sensus fidelium)* knew how to honor a true prophet, while he was threatening to those who had much to protect on the inside. The outsider so consistently has the clear head start in the Scriptures that an insider might almost prefer to be an outsider! It is a very creative tension, "a narrow road that few follow."

But then, even more prophetically, John let go of his popularity and leadership position and pointed beyond himself to one who would not just do the words and the water rite, but would baptize "in Spirit and fire" (Matthew 3:11)—in other words, "the real thing" and not just the ritual. John's glory is that he makes several major transitions that very few people make. He set a pattern of (1) *radical Traditionalism,* which led to (2) *radical critique of the present system,* which led to (3) *the death of his own small self.* There it all is. Jesus would do the exact same thing, and in very real ways it was his cousin who showed him how to do it! John "filled valleys and lowered mountains" and built a "new super highway to God" (Luke 3:5, quoting Isaiah 40:3–5). John the Baptizer is a preliminary icon of the whole necessary passover, that is now called "Christian," yet he was a mainline Jew and a classic biblical prophet. He really is the "precursor," not so much in his message as *in his process and pattern.* His message is largely ambiguous, and not really the point. His life pattern is his message, as is true of Ezekiel, Jeremiah, Jonah, Daniel, Amos and Hosea.

We see curious, anxious and maybe even malicious "priests and Levites" coming down from Jerusalem to observe his private, unorthodox religious rituals at the river (John 1:19–28). They interrogate him at length. We know that John the Baptizer was gathering big crowds and apparently enough to be a bit of a threat to both the religious system and to the political power of Herod, who is trying to keep all control in the family by marrying his brother's wife. *Endogamy,* family dynasty, not adultery, is the primary issue here. Why didn't anyone ever tell us that? Probably our own preoccupation with sexual sin made us read that back into the text. Endogamy was the classic way of not sharing one's power with any other family or person. It was a tyrant solidifying his hold, and explains the ferocity of John's exposure. It is much more a power play within both the temple and royal court that John is exposing than any sexual sin.

A correct use of power is the real theme in John's own life. Will John use his own power and popularity for himself or for others? He passes the test and shows himself to be a man-for-God and a man-for-the-truth, and that is why Jesus can say, "No man born of woman is greater than he" (Luke 7:28). John's verbal and relational skills might not be the best. You would not call him tactful. He is black and white in his thinking, has tunnel vision perhaps, and is even a bit righteous and angry, which is probably why another Bible line says, "The least in the kingdom of God is greater than he is" (Luke 7:29). John is the prophet of the "first half of life spirituality",[1] but he does not represent a second half of life "enlightenment." He willingly and gratefully exits from stage right.

He does not have the ultimate or full message—*but his glory and genius is that he knows that!* He hands it over to one who does.

Observe the bridge that he has built: John, the son of a priestly family from both sides (Luke 1:5) becomes the ultimate embarrassment to his father at work by setting up his own "nature-based" ritual "for the forgiveness" of sin! It is very clear how sins are forgiven through the brokerage house of temple tithes, animal sacrifices and purity laws all administered by the priests, scribes and Levites. No other person in the New Testament has his clothing and eating habits described except John the Baptizer. Why? Because he is clearly a countercultural figure wearing offbeat clothes and eating a non-kosher diet. He is the son of a priest who does not dress like a priest. He is that necessary and good tension that we find between structure and anti-structure, between temple worship and ritual disenchantment. His importance is that he holds them together, and that is why he is such a symbol and bridge builder. *His importance is in his method and mediation between traditional religion and its constant need for radical reform. Somehow he does both, and like always, it gets him killed.* Remember always, when you build a bridge, you will be walked on from both sides (Ephesians 2:14–16), and when you create common ground, you will be "hated by all" (Matthew 10:22). Everybody wants you in their own camp to reassure themselves and to prop up their own game.

The fact that John's countercultural initiation rite was participated in by Jesus himself (see John 3:22) and eventually became normative for the whole Christian tradition, is of itself a pattern that must not be lost. John's very creation of a new initiation rite for adult Jews is a judgment that the old system, for whatever reason, was not working. Maybe not surprisingly, it is the same reason that we are talking about new initiation rites today. For Jesus to cooperate with John's ritual was for Jesus to make the same judgment and to share in his same critique of the temple system.

In some ways, Jesus' death was inevitable too, once he accepted John's baptism. His shocked and withdrawing reaction to John's death seems to indicate that he recognizes the same (Matthew 14:13).

There is always an inherent ritual connection between baptism, anointing and death in the New Testament. If you critique the system publicly, if you refound your life on your divine sonship—accepting another "citizenship" as it were—the system *will* kill you in one way or another. You surely will not fit into citizenship as usual (Philippians 3:20), and you will be consigned to the wilderness, the place for nonconformists and the non-"normal." The only way we could risk calling John a churchy saint was by hushing this all up a bit, sanitizing this wild man and making him into the lovely statue we see in our churches. In this way he neither threatens nor invites anybody.

There is also the interesting "imposing" of the name of John by an angel (Luke 1:13) to Zechariah. His curse of dumbness (1:20–22) is only released after he accepts John's different name. It is clearly a message telling the father to "shut up" and let the boy find his own identity apart from him. This "astonishes" the family. But it could also be seen as a God-given freedom for the child *not* to have to be just like his father! So much ink is spent on this seemingly unimportant incident in Luke that one knows there is something more important going on here (1:5–25, 57–80). The boy is being freed to do what he has to do and to do it outside of the patriarchal and priestly expectation. God has to back him up to do that and separate him from his father's natural control.

Perhaps you could say that his leaping-in-the-womb is a sign of his initiation before the fact—his own "almost immaculate conception" (1:44), as it were. This could easily be seen as a symbol for prenatal Divine identity as something given and not earned or even chosen. It is not dependent on performance or heroics.[2] The very name John means "God is gracious/free" (1:13), and soon this John goes outside his father's temple system and proclaims that

God's forgiveness is as available—as gracious and free—as water in the river (Luke 3:4)! This must have had the religious power brokers rending their garments, while it also made John very popular with the shamed and suffering masses. The church still does not like general or communal confession, except by an occasional begrudged concession.

This is a dangerous man for any religious system and dangerous power for any political system. It is no surprise that they killed John. His head is presented on a platter, as if "food" for the largely unconscious scapegoat mechanism.[3] It is at that point that Jesus "withdraws to a lonely place" and soon reengages full force, creating a "fed and feeding community of workers" (Matthew 14:13f). That is both the power of the martyr to energize the vision and also the power of what we now call "grief work"[4] in Jesus himself.

Finally, it is always a bit disconcerting for Christians to see Jesus taking such a subservient role in relationship to John, submitting to his ritual and his lead. What could this mean if Jesus is in fact the supreme leader? If one sees John merely as the herald of Jesus, it does not make much sense. But if John is actually the initiator of Jesus, and Jesus is modeling for us the correct stance of *beginner's mind,* then it makes perfect sense. The Gospel accounts do connect the water rite as the immediate sending ceremony into the desert "vision quest," and Jesus is assuming the precisely correct posture before his guide. An initiate must be humble, teachable, a novice willing to be guided and taught, a willing beginner. As Jesus himself says to John, "It is fitting to do it in this way, and to follow all that the proper order demands" (Matthew 3:15).

Jesus can therefore initiate us because he himself has been initiated. That is the correct and only pattern for true teachers. Further, it fits the pattern of an older male relative being your initiator. It was never your biological father because that relationship was both too complex and had to be maintained as nurturing.[5] The genius and precociousness of John the Baptist is that he, like Jesus, seems to have "self-initiated" as an adult, since he was also "circumcised on the eighth day" (Luke 1:59) instead of as a teenager. Once I gave a retreat in Ain Karim, and I was taken to the cave of John the Baptist. Local tradition says that John moved there when he was only fourteen years old, just as Jesus abandons his parents at twelve. These boys were early bloomers.

But the most telling thing about the newly discovered baptismal cave of John the Baptist,[6] found nearby, is that there are exactly 28 steps down into the "drowning pool," exactly like the 28 hot rocks that are brought into the Native sweat lodge. These so-called primitive people understood the cyclic death symbolism of 28 and used it for initiation. Every woman knows it every month, but men have to be taught, and it seems that John's original baptism was indeed an initiation into that precise meaning, the necessary cycle of death and rebirth.

Notes

1. Richard Rohr and Paula D'Arcy, *A Spirituality for the Two Halves of Life,* recorded conference, (Cincinnati: St. Anthony Messenger Press, 2004).

2. Claudio Naranjo, *The Divine Child and the Hero: Inner Meaning in Children's Literature* (Canada: Gateways Books and Tapes, 1999). Although these are usually two very different strains in children's literature, John the Baptist is paradoxically presented as both divine child and hero, as is Jesus.

3. Robert G. Hamerton-Kelly, *The Gospel and the Sacred: Poetics of Violence in Mark* (Minneapolis, Minn.: Fortress, 1994), p. 97f.

4. Robert Miller, *Grief Quest* (St. Meinrad, Ind.: Abbey Press, 1996), excellent, short and to the point; Maggie Ross, *The Fountain and the Furnace: The Way of Tears and Fire* (New York: Paulist, 1987), a spiritual favorite of mine on the importance of "tears"; and Thomas R. Golden, *Swallowed by a Snake: The Gift of the Masculine Side of Healing* (Gaithersburg, Md.: Golden Publishing, 2000), is rather convincing that men grieve differently from women.

5. Victor Turner, *The Ritual Process: Structure and Anti-Structure (Lewis Henry Morgan Lectures)* (Ithaca, N.Y.: Cornell University, 1969), p. 119.

6. Shimon Gibson, *The Cave of John the Baptist: The Stunning Archaeological Discovery that has Redefined Christian History* (New York: Random House, 2004).

NINE

Saint Paul as a Master Teacher

You must consider yourselves as dead men brought back to life.

—ROMANS 6:13

Paul was a consummate teacher and initiator himself, which is one reason we have tended *not* to understand him. We prefer the clear moral mandates and the dogmatic clarity that we often need only in the first half of life. We do not want the terrifying journeys, moral ambiguity, process wisdom or the essential but highly mis-understandable truths that Paul usually gives us: "Anyone who relies upon keeping the Law is cursed" (Galatians 3:10). "For me, there are no forbidden things" (1 Corinthians 10:23). "Anything not done in faith is a sin" (Romans 14:23). Or his ambiguous "Pauline Privilege" in regard to marriage and divorce (1 Corinthians 7:15). How do you create an organized religion with hand grenades like that being thrown into the temple?

Paul knows the "one thing necessary," what we now call the paschal mystery, and he is willing to get you there by circuitous routes, along with some essential blows to the imperial mind and arrogant will. He is a "Master" teacher, and we do not understand such teachers anymore.[1] They have too much inner authority because *they know the goal so clearly and do not get sidelined by nonessentials.* As Pope John XXIII put it, "In essentials unity, in nonessentials liberty, and in all things charity." To be honest, Paul's letters would not pass even preliminary orthodoxy tests today, from the Holy Roman Office or the Southern Baptist Convention. Yet, thank God, his letters are considered inspired Scripture.

Paul actually uses the Greek word *memuesmai* ("I have been initiated") only once and in a way that seems to reveal the classic pattern: "I have been through my initiation and now I am ready for anything anywhere; full stomach or empty stomach, poverty or plenty. There is nothing I cannot master with the help of the One who gives me strength" (Philippians 4:12–13). Note the clear "before and after" language. He has many times been led to the edge of his own resources, and gradually learned how to draw his life from the Larger Source, until he can say his marvelous line, "I live no longer not I" (Galatians 2:20). He describes it in many of his letters. That is the key to all initiation.

Paul curiously speaks of himself as "a steward of the mystery...who must be found worthy of the trust....I walk at the end of the procession, with the men sentenced to death" (1 Corinthians 4:1–2, 9). One suspects through several passages like this that he was very familiar with the initiation rites of the mystery religions. They permeated the whole world that he was trying to evangelize. He had to be familiar with them or he would not have known how to talk to his contemporaries in the Hellenized world. His genius and inspiration is that he recognizes Jesus as the new hero who leads us through the needed initiation process *correctly.* In his death-resurrection path, "he who ascended had to first descend, and then he brought gifts to men" (Ephesians 4:8–9). In that one short passage we have a succinct summary of Joseph Campbell's "Monomyth of the Hero," previously referred to, even including the return journey with a "boon" for humanity.

To be a believable hero to the classic and pagan world, *one had to do death right,* and it was Paul's task to present his Jesus as the ultimate hero. Jesus, of course, "does death" in a way that shocks and surprises everybody, even to this day, which makes me think we are still more formed by that classic pagan world, since we do not see how unique Jesus is: contrary to almost all patterns, he does not become the self-serving victim ("playing the victim" to his own self-aggrandizement) nor demand any victimhood of others (which is almost the only story line of history). *Instead, he becomes the forgiving and fruitful victim to awaken us to what we are doing to goodness, to God and to ourselves. He holds, carries, purifies and transforms evil instead of passing it on, like most of us do.* Jesus does death *really right.* He "takes away the sin of the world" by absorbing it himself and exhibits no need to punish anybody else. He transforms the pain instead of transmitting it, and doing that is largely misunderstood to this day. We prefer tit-for-tat morality, passing on the problem, instead of taking away the problem. It fits our small idea of justice, but Paul comes up with a whole new idea of "justification" based entirely on this Jesus pattern of gracious existence.

Jesus lives and teaches redemptive love instead of the common lie of "redemptive violence." This changes everything.[2] He holds the mystery within himself, "pays the price" himself, instead of making others pay the price: "death was at work in him, so that life may be at work in us.…If one man has died for all, then all men should be dead.…This is the new creation" (2 Corinthians 4:11; 5:14, 17). I encourage you to pick up any of Paul's letters and now see if this subtext is not written between the lines of almost his entire body of letters. It is the underlying assumption that makes him ecstatic about Jesus, even though he is a law-abiding Jew. For Paul, Jesus legitimates and makes use of the "groanings" of all creation "in one great act of giving birth" (Romans 8:22). For Paul, Jesus has become the turning point of history, because now everything can be transformed, and most especially, pain. Before

Jesus, it was all about earning and meriting and performing, and Paul knew that would eat us all alive—as it has.

Finally, Paul's account of the eucharistic meal, which is the oldest text of the same that we have, has overtones of the drinking of the blood of the Initiated One and thus entering into solidarity with his bodily journey. This ritual is found in Mythric rites of his time and African initiation rites to this day: "Every time you eat this bread and drink this cup, you are shouting out his death" (1 Corinthians 11:26). He thus introduces the idea of a "memorial meal" that is a "homeopathic cure" for this mystery of death. *Don't fight it or deny it or intellectualize it, but instead "chew on it"! Intoxicate yourself with the blood/wine of the hero until your deaths become one death, and therefore meaningful.* This has become standard eucharistic theology, and I believe was the intention of Jesus, but it has been so prettified, stylized and mass produced, that the typical male never appreciates the graphic, corporeal, sexual and even cannibalistic undertones that are being sung and celebrated. This is revolutionary ritual, especially for Jewish men who could not drink blood under any circumstances (Leviticus 17:14). Why didn't anybody point that out to us?

Paul's theology of the Body of Christ as a community and the Body of Christ as the eucharistic ritual are intrinsically connected, as we see very clearly in 1 Corinthians 11:17–24.[3] The church creates the bread and the bread creates the church, like a wonderful and mutual admiration society. *They mutually recognize and honor God in one another!* This is good theology and a very effective ritual. I see Jesus as absolutely uncompromising about all of this, and it is amazing that any believer would want to water it down: "My flesh is real food and my blood is real drink. He who eats and drinks lives in me and I in him" (John 6:55–56). Or try this one: "Examine yourself to make sure you are in the faith; test yourselves. Do you acknowledge that Jesus Christ is really *in you?* If not, you have failed the test" (2 Corinthians 13:5–6)! The criterion of real faith is very simple for Paul—mutual indwelling—and already now in the flesh—not just later. In this I am quite Catholic and quite orthodox, because that is where all the power for transformation is held, in holding to the incarnation at every level!

I should also point out, however, that Paul is quite eager to distinguish his faith and rituals from the local mystery religions, frankly because there are some similarities. We see this in 1 Corinthians 10:14–22, where he makes clear that our "participation" or communion is with "the blood of Christ" and not with pagan idols, as he puts it. Or when he is quick to distinguish his baptism unto resurrection from the strange rituals of being "baptized for the dead" (1 Corinthians 15:29–34). He is largely working in a Hellenized and initiating world where they could easily be confused. It is a world that defines itself by its rituals, and often rituals of blood, eating and washing. These things are archetypal and universal, and are surely why he can use them so easily among the Gentiles. It is also why they work for us.

The big difference for Paul is that his rituals are promissory notes of the pattern of resurrection and not merely backward looking memorials, as the Mass had become when I was young. I remember growing up in Kansas in the 1950s where most daily Masses were requiem or "black" Masses. In effect the church had become a funereal society, saving the dead instead of liberating the living. But Paul's initiates are initiated into solidarity with Jesus, who has come *from* death. Death is now proclaimed as something triumphed over and walked through. It is dealt with and exposed for the liar that it is: "Death, where is your victory? Death, where is your sting?" (15:56). *Death, for Paul, is neither fate nor fear, but passage and entranceway.* It is the way of dying before you die, just as he did on that road to Damascus and many times thereafter. Thus he is constantly daring death, bragging about overcoming it, and seems to have no fear of it. He is already rejoicing and reveling in resurrection, because it is already alive in him. I love Paul because, in my opinion, he is the first written Christian mystic.

"I will tell you something that has been kept secret. We are not all going to die! But we are changed, instantaneously, in the twinkling of an eye" (1 Corinthians 15:51). Paul speaks with a strange certitude, because it is a past event for him, and not just a future one. He has died more than once, as he himself brags about (2 Corinthians 11), and now he lives a new life—not his own. That is the core, the key and the consummation of all initiation. If many people do not love or appreciate Paul, perhaps it is sometimes because they themselves are not on the other side of death.

Notes

1. Rohr, *Adam's Return*, p. 53f.

2. Rene Girard, *The Girard Reader*, James Williams ed. (New York: Crossroad, 1996).

3. Gunther Bornkamm, *Paul* (San Francisco: Harper & Row, 1971), pp. 188ff., and Samuel Sandmel, *The Genius of Paul: A Study in History* (Minneapolis, Minn.: Fortress Press, 1979), p. 22f, and my own attempt to describe and teach Paul, "The Great Themes of Paul," ten tapes or CDs (Cincinnati: St. Anthony Messenger Press, 2002).

TEN

Man the Money-Maker

Where did the man get this wisdom? Is he not just the son of
a carpenter?

—MATTHEW 13:54

Until the last century, most men who ever lived spent most of their time making and producing things. The majority of men were farmers, planting, cultivating and reaping the fruits of their labors in ways very tangible and down to earth. Many men were also craftsmen and builders. They made things that had form and meaning which made their world livable, which gave it beauty and which enriched the community in which they lived. Men worked with their hands and their heads and their hearts to produce the tangible goods of human culture, and they could see in the products of their work the good they were doing for themselves and others.

In our highly technological society, more and more men are no longer engaged in the traditionally masculine enterprise of making things. Instead, they are engaged in the business of making money, which is finally a mental construct. They move from one job to the next, even from one career to the next, all in the interest of making more money. They have little or no investment in the goods they are making or the services they are offering. Making money is not only the bottom line today, it is the entire ledger. It is also a fictitious product. It is much more a symbol, a projection screen, a status symbol, a lever of power, than anything in and of itself.

This is a drastic shift in the orientation of men vis-a-vis the world they *live* in. A recent survey of boys in the eighth grade of grammar school revealed that 90 percent of them see their primary goal in life as "making lots of money." Not falling in love and raising a family, not inventing or discovering something new, not exploring the secrets of nature, not making the world a better place, not becoming a saint, but simply making money, which is not a real "product" at all. It cannot finally satisfy at a soul level.

In magazines and newspapers I often read stories about men who make small fortunes just by making phone calls or computer transactions. They are playing the stock market or dealing in commodities futures or trading real estate, and in a matter of seconds they are theoretically wealthy, while actually creating nothing for the world, nothing that will last, nothing that is substantial reality, and maybe even entirely for themselves. These men live lives largely outside of the realm of real human relationships, the natural cycle of time and patience, and without ever leaving their own comfort zone. This is a recipe for non-learning. No wonder so many men are emotionally stunted. On the pornographic side, we are actually worried about the percentage of young men who have no need or desire for a real relationship with a real person, because their sexual needs are met entirely on Internet chat lines and porn sites. They have almost no real relational or social skills. This is scary.

It is especially frightening in the area of spirituality. In a very real sense the man who is engaged in making money is not making anything at all. Money is a fiction created to facilitate the exchange of goods and services. It is a something that is really nothing—literally, no thing—except power itself. From the perspective of spirituality, it is an illusion, and very dangerous indeed. Money is a game of numbers used to bolster self-image and to perpetuate a false impression of power. It is the same with phone or Internet sex.

As we have already seen, masculine energy is naturally directed outward. For untold thousands of years that male energy has been directed outward to the world, toward making and producing things, toward creating and sustaining and improving life. In terms of sexuality it can be called phallic energy because one of the basic male drives is toward intercourse and the begetting of further life. The great psychologist, Sigmund Freud, believed that civilization itself was the product of phallic energy that had been sublimated and directed toward things other than sex. Whether or not we agree with Freud, we can see that male sexual energy and male productive energy are both directed outward. My point is that the mere "making of money" is not really directed outward, although it looks like it is. It is first of all directed inward toward self-image, personal security, personal power and private satisfaction.

In today's western culture men's energies are hardly directed toward the creation of life for others and the production of real things, or things they can take pride in. Probably for many of us, the primary example of that is simply the quality of workmanship, the shoddy labor on so many of our products and services, the non-work ethic of many Americans, who seem to want to be paid for doing nothing. I have often agreed with Pope John XXIII who supposedly remarked, when asked about how many people worked at the Vatican, "About half of them." My own dad never missed a day of work at the Atchison, Topeka and Santa Fe for thirty-five years (really!). Now many employees are asking for sick days, vacation days, comp time, retreat time and holidays after two weeks on the job. Maybe even sadder is the willingness to give your whole life producing items of no social benefit, or even destructive, like slot machines, tawdry luxury goods or nuclear weapons. Is that what a man wants to do with his one single chance at life? Money is not just about paying bills, it must also be connected with making some contribution to life, others and history.

Money is an empty symbol precisely because it stands for anything and everything besides the paper or metal it is made of. It stands for me and my importance. Money has no inherent meaning, which is why it can hold any false meaning that we want to put on it. Besides this, the paper and metal in themselves are practically worthless. This then is why directing one's life toward the making of money is so dangerous. It is a life commitment to making what is inherently meaningless and worthless, yet onto it we project all sorts of value and importance.

Up through the Middle Ages in Europe, coins were never a common commodity, and most people simply exchanged goods and services. In the Renaissance, after the invention of printing, paper money made its first appearance. There is an interesting story of how when some friars proudly showed Saint Francis of Assisi some money that had been donated to the order, he took it in his mouth, refused to touch it, walked out to the latrine and dropped it in. Francis saw that it was worthless, but more than that, he wanted to dispel the false impression that by collecting it the friars had done anything to be proud of in itself. Even today, monks in Buddhist monasteries are forbidden to receive gifts of money in any form. They only accept contributions in the form of real things—food, cloth, pottery, wood and so on. Strange to say, but some Buddhists practice the spiritual lesson that Francis wanted to teach, and we Franciscans no longer do.

Please don't get me wrong. I am not advocating that all Franciscans, or all Christians for that matter, should give away all their money and have nothing to do with it. I have money myself, and even a credit card. I am simply pointing out that most great spiritual masters of the past seriously warned against the idolization of money. Jesus makes a quite clear apodictic statement: "You cannot serve both God and money" (Matthew 6:24). Yet that has never been made a central moral teaching, or even a minor one, by either Catholicism or Protestantism.

It is all too easy to fall in love with money, to be captivated by the pursuit of money and to project every manner of meaning and value onto money. If money is not explicitly dethroned, it will never be neutral for long. It will demand allegiance. We make a great deal of the Ten Commandments, yet I wonder if you have ever heard a single sermon in your life on the tenth commandment? As a Catholic, I never have. It is the very name of the main game and would never occur to us as a problem, much less a sin. "Coveting our neighbor's goods" is now called shopping, advertising and contributing to the gross national product (GNP) and the American economy. Amazing how the capital sin of greed can be transmuted into a major virtue.

The book of Ecclesiastes says, "Vanity of vanities, and all is vanity, and mere chasing of the wind....He who loves money, for some reason never has enough of it. He who loves wealth, can never make enough profit... (1:14; 5:9). For some strange reason, I never hear conservative Christians quote lines like that, yet they assure me that they are Bible-based and the word of God is inspired, infallible, inerrant and always true! I am afraid we are dealing with the denial that always covers an addiction.

ELEVEN

Father Hunger

Do you see now that fathers
who cannot love their sons
have sons who cannot love?
It was not your fault
and it was not mine. I needed
your love but I recovered without it.
Now I no longer need anything.

—RICHARD SHELTON[1]

Much of the human race experiences an immense father hunger. It is felt by women, but even more so by men. It seems the same-sex parent has a unique importance in a child's life, and his or her absence leaves a huge, aching hole inside that is never really filled. In all my years in ministry, working in community, leading retreats and giving talks around the world, I have found it to be the single most prevalent absence in the human soul, and also one of the most painful. But the pain is quiet, hidden, denied, and takes many shapes and forms that sons cannot even grasp—or care to grasp.

Once when I was in California giving a series of talks, a young man in his early twenties came up to me in the speaker's lounge and pleaded to talk to me. I invited him to my room and when we got there, he told me his life's story. He started by saying, "It is like a canyon. The chasm between me and my father is like an unpassable canyon."

His father was an engineer. Once when the boy had asked him about God, his father told him bluntly, "Mathematics is my god. If you can't prove it, I cannot talk about it. If it's not logical, I don't believe it." His son was just the opposite, a very sensitive young man, and so he grew up with a stranger for a father. He and his father lived in two different worlds, and their worlds never touched. Nothing life-giving ever passed between them.

As he was telling me his story, I could sense the young man was enjoying, even relishing, the experience. Then suddenly, after about an hour, he just stopped and looked at me.

"You're listening to me!" he said in amazement and near tears. "My dad never once listened to me, but you're listening to me! I feel like I love you!"

We had been really close in that hour, probably closer than that boy had ever been to a man, but I had to leave soon to give another talk. So I prayed with him, holding his hands in mine, for a while longer. Finally, I got up and placed my hands on his head in blessing. "I've got to go now."

"I don't want you to leave," he said desperately.

"But I have to give another talk in a few minutes."

"When you touched me, it felt so good." Then, worried that his words might be misinterpreted, he added, "I'm not gay or anything, but I felt good when you touched me. My father never touched me, or listened to me. Can I come back again?"

The next day, we met again and the same thing happened all over in other ways. He needed someone to tell his feelings to, someone to know who he was, someone to understand the loneliness he felt. He needed someone to affirm and approve him. He needed a father.

Whenever I think about that young man, I realize that he is legion. Thousands and thousands of men, young and old, feel as he does. They grew up without a good man's love, without a father's understanding and affirmation. So they always hunger for it, and they search for it from teachers and coaches, ministers and scoutmasters, and any older man who will offer it to them. Later, in the military or the business world, they seek to be approved by their superiors in exactly the same way. They become the good team players, the good soldiers, who would do anything for the president or the general so long as it meets with his approval. They are the best players in the white male system, corporations, armies or hierarchical churches. They will do almost anything for the assurance and comfort that "Daddy's" approval gives them. It feels like the assurance of God himself. I once had dinner with an old archbishop, and when he would mention cardinals or the pope, his voice would actually become hushed with boyish admiration for what he called "the princes of the church." He did not have much real father energy himself because he was still looking for it in others.

I meet father hunger in many different settings. For fourteen years I was the chaplain at the Albuquerque jail, which is a very macho Hispanic subculture all its own. Often the prisoners interact with one another or with the guards with a great display of machismo with all the usual hardness and acting tough. But often when one of them is alone with me, the whole picture changes. They are little boys anxious to please, and in their comforted state, where they no longer have to perform, I am *Padrecito,* the dear little father. I can remember one man who came to see me. He was well built and had a tattoo of Our Lady of Guadalupe on one arm and a naked lady on the other. "Look, Father, I can make them move," he said, flexing his muscle. In his eyes I saw a little boy, trying to get daddy's attention, and so safe that both sexuality and spirituality could be expressed as one. That's what young men want from an older man.

Many times prisoners will make excuses just to be alone and talk. They will ask to go to confession even though they sometimes have little to confess. But they bring up anything, hoping it is a big enough sin, just so they could tell me about their inner lives and their private selves. After hearing a prisoner's confession, I always lay my hand on his head or shoulder as I give him my blessing. Invariably, if I touch him, he cries. He hangs his head down, so I won't see the tears in his eyes, but there he is, sobbing like a little boy needing to be held and hugged. He would never do that, of course. Father hunger is a great gaping wound that many carry, without realizing it or, at least, without being able to name it. It is a deprivation that many are constantly trying to overcome, a need that they are always seeking to satisfy. A very high percentage of fathers in history were killed in war, absent at work, alcoholic, abusive or just emotionally unavailable or uninterested in their children. Some were rejected or abandoned by fathers; some were second or third in their minds to a preferred brother or sister.

Our father, and his response to us, is the first response of an "outsider." Mom's love is body-based from the womb and the breast. It is assumed, taken for granted, relied upon instinctively, which is why a foundational "mother wound" can be even more devastating to one's very core. When one's good mother dies, it first feels like God has died, because she is your first clear God image and Divine security.

But Dad is that other one in the house, at a greater distance. He does not "have" to love you. His love is not inherently and instinctively felt and drawn upon, like Mother love. He must *choose* to love you! He decides for you, he picks you out, he notices you among the many. It redeems, liberates and delights, therefore, in a totally different way. As we know, God was first seen as feminine by almost all primal cultures, but then Jewish religion also came to see God as "Abba," Father, Daddy, because their experience was of being chosen by God, being the objects of Divine Election, being personally preferred to the other nations. "When Yahweh set his heart on you and chose you, it was not because you were greater than other peoples, you were the least of all the peoples. It was simply for love of you that Yahweh chose you" (Deuteronomy 7:7). That is the uniquely transformative experience of male love. It validates us and affirms us deeply, precisely because it is not necessary. It is totally free love, non-needy, non-manipulative, non-codependent—and only such love finally feels like love at all. Of course, a good mother loves in that way, too.

It is my conviction that this healing is what Judeo-Christianity was trying to communicate in seeming to prefer masculine metaphors for God. We know that God is neither masculine nor feminine, and we must continue to use feminine images for God, too, but the father wound is so deep and so pervasive in much of the world and much of history, that *even Jesus needed to use the more daring, the more distant and the more dangerous word for God—"Abba"—because that is where the wound lies for so many.* That is where the deep healing will happen, and must happen. In fact, the very people who most want to throw out the masculine word entirely are usually people who themselves have a distant or denied relationship with the masculine. They are missing out on at least half of the mystery of God if they hate and reject the word "Father" and the meaning behind it. Many conservatives, who hate the word "Mother" for God, are also missing out on at least half of the mystery of God. If they are Catholic, they try to compensate by a near adoration of Mary, who becomes all the things they fear the Father God is not: merciful, nurturing, forgiving and tender. A simple rule of thumb is this: the more macho and distant the male is in any particular Catholic country, the more they will substitute Mary for any Scripture-based Christianity. Protestants tend to get just more moralistic to please the demanding Father God, and they do not even understand any mystical or spousal Christianity.

It is not a matter of gender wars, or feminine affirmative action, it is a matter of all of us finding the words and images that break us through to love! If you have a mother wound, you probably deeply need feminine metaphors for God. If you are a gay man, it will be male images that will fascinate your soul and open your heart. If you have been rejected or abandoned by men, it will be an accepting male image that you will most hate and fear and need, and it is precisely there that you will one day be brought to your knees and to tears. In the whole of our life, of course, we eventually need to be loved by both the Divine feminine and the Divine masculine, which is to be fully "born again"! God is great enough and whole enough to give us both. We hunger for a perfect love.

It seems that we cannot be ourselves, we cannot be our own man, or our own father, until we have been someone else's little boy. We need him to like us, to bless us even after our mistakes, to enjoy our company, to tell us that we can succeed. The separation from the one who is the same as us (our father) is somehow even more destructive than the separation from the one who is opposite (our mother). If manhood itself does not like me, then I'm forever insecure about my own. His affirmation is ten times more important than that of any other man, and of a completely different quality than the affirmation of a woman. Until and unless we get it, every male relationship will somehow be our unmet father, for good or for ill.

Just how destructive is father hunger? How far could a man go to satisfy the need for approval denied by his father? What might he do to release his suppressed anger?

The German psychologist Alice Miller wrote a study about a man who had been abused as a child. His father beat him for every little infraction, real or imaginary. He wouldn't even call his son by name. When he wanted the boy to come to him, he whistled for him, as if the boy were a dog. Hatred seethed within the boy, but he could not vent his anger on his father. He kept it within, nursing it. Then, some time later, the son discovered that his grandfather (of whom he knew little) had been Jewish. His distorted thinking led him to believe that this Jewish blood was the reason for his father's behavior. The boy's name was Adolph Hitler. You already know the rest of his destructive story.[2]

It is what we do not know immediately and personally that we will often hate and fear the most. The unknown grandfather of Hitler becomes evil incarnate, the absent father of the black boy becomes the hated policeman on the street, the abusive and disconnected Hispanic father creates sons who abuse and dominate all others. The son whose father died young confuses his father hunger with sexual desire and allows himself to be abused.

But the absent one can also create holy desire and holy longing. Father hunger can work both ways. Some men for some reason, it must surely be grace, fill that hole with the visions and images and ideals of a thousand other men that they meet along the way. Many of the greatest, kindest and most effective men I have ever met were driven to their life's task by an aching father hunger that they often did not recognize themselves. It led them to be good students to mentors, help other boys, befriend other men, to nurture themselves because they had not been nurtured. But most especially they sometimes learn to seek, to desire and to trust that God is that loving and compassionate Daddy they always wanted. And that's exactly what Jesus told us was true in his favorite story that we call the Prodigal Son (Luke 15:11–32).

Notes

1. Richard Shelton, "Letter to a Dead Father" in *Brother Songs: A Male Anthology of Poetry,* Jim Perlman, ed. (Minneapolis, Minn.: Holy Cow Press, 1979), p. 21.

2. Alice Miller, *For Your Own Good: Hidden Cruelty in Child Rearing and the Roots of Violence* (New York, N.Y.: Farrar, Straus & Giroux, Inc., 1983), pp. 142–197.

TWELVE

The Father Wound

Three things are to be feared and hated: earthquakes, fires, and fathers.

—A Japanese aphorism

Father hunger often becomes a full-blown father wound. Some use that term to highlight the woundedness in a man's psyche that results from not having a father—whether it is because the father has died or left the family, because the father's work keeps him absent from the scene most of the time or because the father keeps himself aloof from involvement with his children. In any event, the result is a deep hurt, a deprivation that leads to a poor sense of one's own center and boundaries, a mind that is disconnected from one's body and emotions, a life often with the passivity of an unlit fire.

When I was giving a retreat in Peru in 1977, a sister who ministers in Lima's central prison brought this lesson home to me. She described how, as Mother's Day was approaching during her first year there, the men in the prison kept asking her for Mother's Day cards. She kept bringing boxes and boxes of cards for the prisoners to send to mama, but she never seemed to have enough. So as Father's Day approached, she decided to prepare for the onslaught of requests by buying an entire case of Father's Day cards. But that case, she told me, is still sitting in her office. Not one man asked her for a Father's Day card. She couldn't even give them away.

She realized then—and as she told me this story with tears in her eyes—that most of the men were in jail because they had no fathers. Not that they were orphans, but they had never been fathered. They had never seen themselves as sons of men who admired them, they had never felt a deep secure identity, they had never received that primal enthusiasm that comes from growing up in immediate contact with an older and secure man. And so they spent their lives trying to become men in devious and destructive ways. They were insecure men who had to prove that they were men, *because no one ever told them that they were.* Their negative acting out invariably became acts of lawlessness, opposition and violence.

Not having reached the deep masculine within them, they look to other men for assurance and affirmation. The gang phenomenon takes many forms, but it is usually an exercise in futility, seventeen-year-old boys trying to get father energy from other seventeen-year-old boys. Not having found that inner strength which gives them a sense a good ego structure, they are constantly trying to prove who they are. Whether they engage in "macho" games of physical fitness, sexual prowess or business success, they desperately need to show themselves and others that they have made it and that they are really men. But their continuous running from one accomplishment to another only proves that they have not made it, which is the only place that really counts. Not having found their self-worth, they try to prove their value by accumulating things or money or exercising power. But their constant search for *earned worth,* which is a certain contradiction in terms, betrays their inner sense of worthlessness.

Jean Vanier, the founder of many L'Arche communities for the handicapped and retarded around the world, once told me at their headquarters in France, that he found very few men who did not suffer from two wounds: wounds to their sexuality and wounds in relationship to authority. I gasped back at him, "That is exactly my experience"! Almost every man in western society suffers from some sexual wound.[1] It bleeds excruciatingly in sexual violence toward women, addiction within themselves and homophobia toward other men. I have never once had a man tell me that he felt his sexuality was whole, healthy and happy. It always seems to be a cross, a dilemma, a shame, a fear, a doubt or an impossible desire. Sexual issues are always at the heart of masculine spirituality. It must be tapped for good, or it will always be the "thorn in the flesh" that keeps men paralyzed, addicted and living double lives. Basically, I think we need to have healthy sexuality modeled for us by our fathers, or we all start at zero and make all the same mistakes generation after generation.

A high percentage of men also have problems with authority. They are either on bended knee before it, which we see in most conservatives, or in constant reaction against it, which we see in most liberals. It almost defines the political and ecclesiastical landscape. If we have not encountered a man with true inner authority, we allow authority to be something external and arbitrary, and we either love it or hate it at that level. But both miss the point. Since they have not experienced the spiritual and inner authority gained from authentic God experience, they either look for it externally or fight it externally. Authority for them is never inner wisdom but usually outer obligation. That is the way they experience authority, so that is the way both will invariably exercise authority—either over-needing it (most conservatives) or abdicating it (most liberals). Neither of them have usually integrated or even found that calm place which allows you to do that delicate and mature dance between both inner and outer authority.

In doing so, however, they create problems for themselves and others. Just imposing your will engenders both obedience and passivity, both compliance and resentment, both surface respect and hidden rage. Thus, most men perpetuate the very system that keeps them imprisoned—whether they are locked into being subordinates or superiors. Mere outer authority gets the job done at a certain level, but both parties remain reactionary to one another, and remain stunted at that level of relationship.

Even though there are no guarantees in life, we can help our own sons by sharing our inner lives with them, our thoughts, feelings, dreams and hurts. One psychologist told me that most boys lose their respect for their fathers by the time they reach sixteen. I suppose it is somewhat normal for adolescents to want to break the parental bond around that age. How healthy or unhealthy the break is, however, depends a lot on the quality and style of our fathering. If we have neglected or bullied our sons in their boyhood, the break will be an abandonment of some sort, or a rebellion that may never be healed. But if we have affirmed and challenged them into manhood, and shared our own struggles with them, the break will be a loosening of the parent-child relationship that in time will be rebonded in a man-to-man relationship. It is more important to draw our sons into a process with us than to give them too-neat conclusions.

Our sons are not stupid. If they've received good masculine energy from their dads as they were growing up, they're not going to reject it when they've grown. If they've learned to trust the masculine during their boyhood, they'll be able to trust it in us and find it in themselves during their manhood. They may look for affirmation and models elsewhere—among their peers, their teachers and coaches, their real or fictional heroes—but that is normal. No man can be everything, even to his own son, who has to build his own manhood by incorporating parts of many role models into his own adult self. But no smart son will discard the example that his father gave him if what he received was an honest, loving experience of his father and a healthy sense of himself as a man.

A son needs to believe that his father respects and even admires him. I always say that men are very simple creatures. *All most men require is respect!* As a boy he wants his daddy to be proud of him, but as he grows toward manhood a father's pride can seem very patronizing to him. What he needs all along is not only parental approval but an adult's respect and honest admiration. If dad waits until junior's a teenager, it's too late. *That honoring of the man in the boy is what invites the boy to join the club of men.* That honoring is what lets him know that he is finally his father's equal, that he and the father are one. Yet sons usually admit that a part of them needs and wants to keep dad on a pedestal forever, they need and want him to be their dad and not a total peer. (I recall the deep disappointment and confusion felt by one young man I knew when his dad got on his knees in front of him and confessed his sexual secrets and irresponsible lifestyle to him.)

The father wound is so deep and so all-pervasive in so many parts of the world that its healing could well be the most radical social reform conceivable. I am convinced that this distortion lies at the bottom of much crime, militarism, competitive greed, pathological need for leaders and family instability. What can we do to heal this wound? I suggest three simple ways to struggle toward healing of the father wound.

First, we must work through the hurts we feel to an adult and forgiving relationship with our own fathers and father figures. Second, we must nurture and perhaps seek reparenting of our little boy within, through healing prayer, male relationships and perhaps some inner spiritual work with the help of a counselor or therapist. And, finally, we should dedicate some of our own father energies to reforming destructive patriarchal structures in our society and to nurturing and healing the next generation of men.

Let me end with a reference to Saint Francis of Assisi, who had a deep father wound. His father seems to have verbally, if not physically, abused him as a young man, perhaps thinking Francis and his mother were too close (which is a common phenomenon with eldest or sensitive sons who bond deeply with the mother). This only got worse when Francis as a young man set out on his spiritual quest, seemingly rejecting his father's success, business and worldview.

We have one telling story from the early life of Saint Francis, which seems to reveal how much this rupture hurt Francesco all of his life, and his own creative use of what we would call "psycho-drama" to heal this gnawing wound.

Much of his later life, Francis lived in the plain below Assisi, in what is called the Portiuncula, where he first worked with the lepers and then gathered his community of friars. On occasion when Francis would walk up the hill to town, he would deeply fear encountering his father in the streets, who would often curse him and reject him again as his son.

Francis undoubtedly carried a bit of guilt about his own dramatic and showy rejection of his father in the city square many years previously. He undoubtedly recognized there was still a lot of ego in that, when he publicly shamed his human father in his youthful search for the heavenly father. A mature saint would not have done that. He now knew better, but he could not repair the utterly broken relationship.

At any rate, that continual rejection from his father hurt so much that Francesco would invite a beggar from the streets to accompany him, walk by his side and protect his soul. He instructed him, "When my father hurls curses and abuse at me, I will hear them painfully in one ear, but I ask you to walk on my other side, and whisper God's favor into my other ear, 'Francis, you are my beloved son. You are a son of heaven and a son of God.' Just keep repeating it until I can believe it again!" That alone could save him from the sour and sad heart that a father's rejection forever bestows on a son.[2]

Scholars have been unable to find a single reference or allusion to this relationship ever being publicly reconciled, even though Francis, according to the Smithsonian Library, has the longest list of books written about him of any man or woman in human history! Maybe he is so universally loved and admired precisely because he was so ordinary, human, wounded and patched up, just like all the rest of us.

Now if the great Saint Francis of Assisi bore his father wound that heavily and long lastingly, we know how deep that wound can be. We see that he created rituals of healing for himself, and surely forgave his father and asked for his forgiveness. It also might have been the underlying hurt that drove him toward his passionate search for God, his desire for a perfect and always accepting Father. His wound became his sacred wound, which then does not seem like a wound at all.

Notes

1. Eugene Kennedy, *The Unhealed Wound: The Church and Human Sexuality* (New York: St. Martin's Press, 2001.)

2. "Legend of the Three Companions," #23, *St. Francis of Assisi Writings and Early Biographies: English Omnibus of the Sources for the Life of St. Francis,* Marion A. Habig ed. and R. Brown, B. Fahy, P. Hermann, P. Oligny, N. de Robeck, L. Sherley-Price, trans. (Chicago, Ill.: Franciscan Herald Press, 1973).

THIRTEEN

Grief Work

Be still and wait without hope, for hope would be hope for the wrong thing.

—T.S. ELIOT, "East Coker" from the *Four Quartets*

Most men grow up with an emptiness inside them. Call it father hunger, call it male deprivation, call it personal insecurity, it's the same emptiness. When positive masculine energy, a male mode of feeling is not modeled from father to son, it creates a vacuum in the souls of men. And into that vacuum demons pour. Among other things, they seem to lose the ability to know how to read situations and people correctly. There is little confidence in their own human judgments or ability to relate personally. That is a huge loss. Men do not know what they really feel, how to empathize with the feelings of others, and most especially they do not know how to cry.

While not qualified to play the psychologist here, I just want to use this crucial and defining emptiness in men, as a takeoff for why children need to be raised by both mothers and fathers, in order to find their true and best selves. I am convinced there is a "male" way of feeling, a male way of grieving,[1] that is needed to balance out our male way of thinking. Without it, we become very split and one-sided, but women cannot teach us a healthy male way of feeling. We need a man to do that for us.

I once read a study of children who were raised by their fathers at home while their mothers went off to work. The report referred to them as "superkids" because almost all of them succeeded in childhood and adulthood far above the statistical average. No doubt their success in life was due to a number of factors, not the least of which is that they had parents who were creative and free enough that they could successfully reverse the traditional parenting roles in our society. But I suspect, too, that the father's love, which has a different quality about it than the mother's love, had a lot to do with them being "superkids." Positive masculine energy, whether from the father or the mother, has the power to give children great self-confidence and assurance.

Speaking from my own experience, I can truthfully say that one of the reasons I became a priest is that my father always believed in me. Whenever I was tempted to doubt myself, or wonder if I was up to trying something, he told me he was sure that I could do it. I never grew up with many problems of self-doubt that I see in so many young people I've worked with. Sure, I was also my mother's eldest and beloved son, and her love utterly grounded me, but Dad's love "sent" me into the bigger world. It is no wonder that those Jesus affirmed were called the "sent ones" or apostles. That's what men do for men. They give one another energy for life, and especially life in the outer world. It is the old roots and wings metaphor: mother love roots us in our souls, ourselves and our bodies; father love allows us to do something good with all those wonderful roots. It teaches us to fly.

When a father tells a child that he can do something, he can do it. I don't know why that is, except to say that there is some mysterious energy that passes from the male to his children. Sometimes it can even be foolhardy, like when I went to swim seven laps for a merit badge when I was fourteen, never having swum seven laps even once, but Daddy told me I could do it! (I failed.) Father energy is some sort of creative energy that can make things be when they are not, and without which things cannot come to be. When male energy is absent, creation does not happen, either in the human soul or in the world. Nurturance happens, support and love happen, which is the wonderful feminine gift, but not that new "creation out of nothing" that is the unique prerogative associated with the masculine side of God.

Without the father's energy, there is a void, an emptiness in the soul which nothing seems to be able to fill. All of the predictable wounds of failure and rejection wound deeply because there is no one to hold them, carry them with us, purify them and transform them. As we get older, we just get deeply sad. *It is sadness, but it shows itself as anger.* For men to recognize that one aspect of themselves is often the beginning of major transformation, self-discovery and even self-compassion. Most men do not know that they are really sad, and their lives are filled with unfinished hurt. They found ways to get rid of the pain before they really "suffered" it and learned its good lessons. Many men think they are angry, but most male anger is really hidden sadness. To resolve this disconnect, almost all initiation rites had to teach young men how to weep.

The importance of this became clear to me in my studies of the universal phenomena of male initiation rites. These rites almost always included a period of what we would call "grief work" or exercises in bereavement, the necessity for the male to join in with "the tears of things." Perhaps it was a way of protecting his soul in what was almost always a harsh and brutal world. Yet tears do not seem to come naturally to most males. He had to be taught, what Jesus also taught, that "those who weep are blessed" (Matthew 5:5). I suspect that non-weeping is a price that the male has had to pay for centuries of going to war (which is almost the one single norm of history), leaving home so young to fight for things that he barely understood. You have to split, deny and repress your feeling world to survive such ordeals. In effect, we have chosen the survival of cultural and nationalistic pretenses over the survival of the male soul. Yes, men are often warlike, but they have been bred like dogs to do it, over-developing some qualities like detachment and stoicism, and repressing others like feeling, empathy and vulnerability. Initiation tried to still keep them in some kind of balance.

You see, the "grieving mode" is quite different than the fixing mode, the controlling mode or even the understanding mode of life. The male had to be shown how to live and feel grief, or he would spend all his life in these other three, which is what has largely happened. Grief, as I define it, is simply *unfinished hurt.* It seems to need to go through all of its laborious stages. Hurt is never just over and gone. It is a process of letting go, suffering our loss, feeling it deeply and allowing it to change us. And perhaps it changes us like almost nothing else. Women seem to learn staging through their twenty-eight-day cycle and their nine-month gestation period. We men have no such learning curve.

Grief, it seems, makes us more permeable, where we can get out of ourselves and others can get in. It actually changes the very shape of our soul. That is why we *must* experience loss and emptiness, we must practice letting go of things, we must suffer death to be able to enjoy life. Without grief work, and it is *work,* over an extended time, the soul remains self-enclosed, rattling around inside its own limited logic and basically disconnected from the rest of the world.

If men are not led through the stages and experiences of grief, which will always feel like dying, they end up suffering even more through the neurotic pains of aimless depression, desperation, various forms of addiction and even suicidal temptations. Who, tell me who, will teach you this, when even the church does not do it? Christianity has made the crucifixion itself into a mechanical atonement theory instead of the necessary message of transformation, the price of all true love. As Carl Jung said, and I paraphrase him, we either face the legitimate pain of being human, or we bring on ourselves a destructive pain that is ten times worse. Grief work taught men how to carry the suffering of legitimate pain, which process itself then became an even greater teacher. Do not get rid of your hurts until you have learned all that they have to teach you. When you are in the middle of them, I warn you that you will need a coach who has been there himself first.

We have chosen Jonah emerging from the belly of the whale as our logo for our M.A.L.Es (Men as Learners and Elders) program, precisely because grief and darkness are at the heart of authentic men's work. Much of early men's work is teaching men how to trust their time in the belly of the whale, how to stay there without needing to fix, to control or even to fully understand it, and to wait until God spits you up on a new shore. It is called "liminal space," and I believe all in-depth transformation takes place inside of liminal space. To hope too quickly is to hope for the wrong thing. The belly of the whale is the great teaching space, and thus it is no surprise that Jesus said that "the sign of Jonah was the only sign he was going to give" (Luke 11:30). In fact, it would be an "adulterous" generation that would seek any other sign. Men must learn how to grieve, or they are inevitably angry and controlling, and they don't even know why.

Note

1.   Golden, *Swallowed by a Snake.*

FOURTEEN

Three Kinds of Men

On the sabbath he went into the synagogue and taught, and there was a man whose right hand was withered. The scribes and Pharisees watched him closely to see if he would cure on the sabbath so that they might discover a reason to accuse him. But he realized their intentions and said to the man with the withered hand, "Come up and stand before us." And he rose and stood there. Then Jesus said to them, "I ask you, is it lawful to do good on the sabbath rather than to do evil, to save life rather than to destroy it?" Looking around at them all, he then said to him, "Stretch out your hand." He did so and his hand was restored. But they became enraged and discussed together what they might do to Jesus.

—LUKE 6:6–11

In this story there are three kinds of men. The man with the withered hand is one kind of man, the scribes and Pharisees are another, and the man Jesus is a third kind. We can learn a great deal about ourselves by looking at these three kinds of men and asking ourselves where we might be if we were in the story.

The man with the withered hand is typical of so many men in the world today. Notice that it is his *right* hand that is withered. That's the functional hand, the producing hand. This man is an image of those who are incapable of achieving what they desire or accomplishing what they would like to happen.

He is weak. He just happens to be there in the synagogue, sitting somewhere. He doesn't have any initiative or determination. He doesn't ask for anything. He doesn't even ask to be cured, as many do in the healing stories in the Gospels. Instead, Jesus has to call him. And when Jesus does call him, he stands there silently. He does what Jesus tells him to do, but we never hear a word from him the whole time. Even after he is cured, he does not thank Jesus or praise God or tell others about it. He does not make life happen, he waits for others to make it happen, and then *perhaps* reacts. He is not going anywhere with his life, and he doesn't even care that he's not going anywhere. It is precisely this kind of man that is so disappointing to a son.

The description fits all too many men today, not only in our American culture but in much of the world today. Most men do not know how to motivate themselves. If they have any motivation at all, it is for some form of immediate money, sex or power. Nothing more. They have no internal motivation, and without the external motivations of money, sex and power they do not know how to choose or make decisions about what they want to do with their lives.

Another way to say this is that most men have no interior juice and joy. They need something outside (like a law or fear) to kick them, to get them going, to offer them security, to promote them, to reward them, to make them momentarily "happy." Spirituality is a matter of having a source of energy within which is a motivating and directing force for living.

The incident in Luke's Gospel is often called a healing story, but I myself wonder whether he is really healed. Maybe his hand is working again, but nothing else seems to be working. Those of us who have had experience in the healing ministry of the charismatic movement, or who have witnessed healings through the sacramental anointing of the sick, know the importance of psychological and emotional follow-through. If a physical healing is not accompanied by spiritual healing, the physical symptoms of the illness often return. Physical healing is always a call to inner change, a change of heart, a change of direction. After he healed people, Jesus often told them to get up and walk, or to go and sin no more. There is no indication in this story that the man ever does anything like this. In response to Jesus' miraculous intervention, he just stands there.

The scribes and the Pharisees represent another kind of man in the world today. In the story, ironically, they are church people. They take religion seriously, yet they are trying to block the work of God. They are involved with religion, yet they want nothing to do with healing, freedom or the giving of life. They are trapped in their heads, caught up in their moral principles, blinded by their doctrines. They watch from a distance, critically observing what is going on, in order to accuse. They are men of ill will, but ill will carefully disguised. The best way to be a hateful person and not to feel an ounce of guilt about it is to be hateful for God.

They are what we might call "power conservatives," holding on to the position and security that institutional religion gives them. Such men are very different from "value conservatives," or people who hold on to the truly traditional values of the gospel. Under the guise of religious values, what they are really into is power and control. They are not just in the Catholic church but in Protestant denominations, as well as in Judaism and Islam. They are the ambitious spokespeople of religious power, and they use God as a front for their own need for control. When they are questioned, as Jesus questions the scribes and Pharisees, they are silent, they deny, or they put up a smoke screen. They are full of indignation, but they do not betray their true motives to anyone, not even to themselves.

Another thing to notice about these men in the story is that they think and act as a group. They are not individuals but repre-sentatives of a sort of groupthink, which in this case is religiosity.

It might also be patriotism or capitalism or some sort of ethnic chauvinism. Whatever it is, it is opposed to individual consciousness and personal conscience. Collectivist thinking is one of the cheapest and most common substitutes for personal growth and mature conscience. The Pharisees represent the need for propriety and social control, a very common form of first-stage morality. True conscience and the risks of integrity are beyond their understanding and usually are a serious threat to them. It is amazing that the villains in most of Jesus' stories are religious people.

Finally, we see the man Jesus. In five short verses this one man enters, teaches, recognizes what others are thinking, commands, questions and calmly acts. He faces his accusers without panic because he knows what they are thinking. He speaks with inner authority when he addresses the other two kinds of men. He is not afraid to confront people or to question the law. He knows what he is about to do and he does it. He doesn't explain. He doesn't take credit. He doesn't ask for recognition. *He just does the truth and he bears their silent fury.* He holds and carries the tension and does not return it in kind. In fact, he has turned their hatred into healing. He transforms pain instead of transmitting it.

When Jesus leaves the scene, he goes off into the hills to pray and, after that, he gathers his little community together:

> In those days he departed to the mountain to pray, and he spent the night in prayer to God. When day came, he called his disciples to himself, and from them he chose Twelve, whom he also named apostles. (Luke 6:12–13)

Being in a hostile situation, being face-to-face with people who hate you, takes a heavy toll on a man. Living in a negative environment, whether it is at home or at work, is spiritually draining. Jesus recognizes this, and so he finds a way to brace himself against the negativity and debilitating energy of toxic people.

We must never be afraid to do the same. The wise warrior (the part of a man who protects his own boundaries appropriately) moves out of the ugly situation created by his accusers and away from the spiritual weakness of the man he helped, in order to gather his own spiritual strength.

He finds it, first of all, in communion with God. But he makes it happen, secondly, by forming a new community around himself. He will teach them that there is a new way of living besides the ways represented by the other two kinds of men. He will show them that there is a new way of understanding what is going on in the world and a new way of acting in the face of power and paralysis. Remember, we do not think ourselves into new ways of living, but we live ourselves into new ways of thinking. Jesus moves toward lifestyle solutions and not academic ones.

Jesus forms a healthy community of men as a living alternative to the dysfunctional ways that men usually organize themselves. The church was supposed to be that alternative society, it was intended to be God's "new world order." But if you cannot find that Jesus energy in your church or parish, gather with a group of honest brothers who can protect you from and affirm you in something other than passivity (the withered hand) and negativity (scribes and Pharisees). You cannot do it alone.

FIFTEEN

1 and the Father Are One

I fled him, down the nights and down the days;
I fled him down the arches of the years;
I fled him, down the labyrinthine ways
Of my own mind; and in the mist of tears
I hid from him.

—FRANCIS THOMPSON, "The Hound of Heaven"[1]

In the Gospel of John, in speaking about his relationship with God, Jesus emphasizes that he and the Father are one (John 10:30). Jesus repeats this theme again and again as though rejoicing in his relationship as Son to the Father, and even more, as if it is his basic identity, almost his very name. We think he is doing some free advertising for himself, but of course, he is also talking about us! He is *the icon of all of us.* He is everyman. Jesus believes the paradox that we only intuit, desire and utterly hope for—that we could also be both human and divine, both a son of earth and a son of heaven. And, of course, we are but don't know it. He did.

As we have seen, however, most men, like Francis Thompson above, would say, "I and my father are *not* one." This alienation between sons and fathers is a major reason why many men become either powerless or power-wielding, instead of calmly holding their power like Jesus.

93

The American poet Robert Bly believes that this father-son alienation has not always been as intense as it is today. Although we cannot assume that down through the ages all men had happy and wholesome relationships with their fathers, he points to a number of factors which suggest that prior to the industrial revolution most men had much closer relationships with their fathers than they have had since.[2]

Before the industrial revolution, Bly observes, boys commonly grew up in a close working relationship with their fathers. They worked on the family farm or in the family business along with their fathers, learning to be farmers or craftsmen or businessmen and made a real contribution to their family's well-being. From the beginning of their lives, therefore, boys grew up with the understanding that they were part of their father's world and that they were important. They did not have to wonder about their identity, or even search for it, because they already had it. And they did not have to earn society's approval later in life because they already had their father's approval, which was all that mattered.

In the nineteenth century, however, men in great numbers left the farms and went to work in factories, and in the twentieth century more and more men left family businesses to work in the office buildings of large corporations. By and large, their sons had immediate access to neither of these worlds. I never once saw where my own father worked in the shops of the Atchison, Topeka and Santa Fe Railroad. During the last century and a half, the majority of boys have had to grow up without close contact with their fathers and without the assurance that they had a place in the world of men.

The result is what I have already characterized as father hunger, or a deep need for masculine acceptance and approval. But the result, according to Bly, is even more far-reaching than that. In addition to the need for a father figure, boys grow up lacking many of the attitudes and perceptions they almost spontaneously acquire when they mature in the company of men. For lack of a male role model, they are uncomfortable in their own role as men. Not seeing how their fathers relate to their feelings, they are awkward with their own feelings. Not seeing how their fathers relate to other men, they lack independence and self-assurance. They tend to be either very submissive to authority or very resentful of authority because, not having learned early on how to trust and work with their fathers in an ongoing partnership, they do not have a healthy conception of authority.

I myself didn't fully appreciate the impact that this change in the father-son relationship has had on men until I was invited to speak in countries outside the United States. In those parts of Africa that are still largely rural and agricultural, for example, I was profoundly impressed by the way that boys who grow up in their tribal villages carried themselves. Although they might lack some other qualities, they often walked and operated with a kind of self-confidence that I don't see in many grown men in our society. Even in their thirties and forties, most American men are still trying to make it as men, pursuing the tokens of manhood in power, possessions and prestige. In preindustrial Africa, though, boys often move with the self-assurance of men because they do not have to earn their worth as we do. It is bestowed on them by their fathers.

I found the exact opposite in Jamaica, where the traditional family and way of life were destroyed first by actual slavery and later by economic slavery. In that supposedly tropical paradise, men are forced to leave their families to work as field hands or in resorts where they do not make enough for their families to join them. They have to live in company shacks or run-down apartments with other men, and they can go home to their wives and children in the countryside only once a week or a few times a month. The same is true in South Africa.

In Jamaica, during most of the talk that I was giving, I could hear a general rustling of people talking and moving about in the rather large crowd. Then, when I began to speak about the importance of fathering in families, the noise gave way to dead silence. I could tell that my words had touched these people at a very profound level. I was naming something that they were feeling and acknowledging deep within themselves—a suffering and a longing for fathering. Few of them had grown up with a father at home, a father who could be there when they needed him. All of them had experienced the pain of never having really known their fathers.

Although most men in our own country grow up without a strong presence of a father in their life, I never saw how far absent fatherhood can go in an industrial society until I visited Japan. The Japanese are raised almost entirely by their mothers, even more than we are. Child rearing is considered women's work, something beneath a man's dignity. As a result, young Japanese boys at home grow up in a female-dominated environment, especially in the big cities.

Japanese men do not like to come home for supper with their families. They stay at work in the factory or office long into the evening, to demonstrate their loyalty to the company and their boss. Their father figure is their supervisor, so they work very hard and spend long hours to please him. They dare not leave work until after the boss has left, and then they go out to have supper with other men.

On a typical evening in Tokyo, the restaurants are filled with throngs of men getting together to unwind from the pressures of the day, to complain and let off steam and to celebrate whatever successes they've had on the job, instead of going home to be with their wives and children. It seemed so evident to me, as I watched them, that they were playing the roles of father and son to each other—assuring and being affirmed, complimenting and being praised, giving advice and asking for it. What they never gave or received at home, they were seeking in the workplace from other men. Soon, they go to the bars to drink saki together, or else they go to the baths to soak and steam with other men. Finally, around ten or eleven at night, they start leaving the city, and the subways are filled with silent and sometimes drunken men, going home to sleep. This male emptiness breeds tremendous needs for conformity and acceptance by other men. In Japan most men dress alike, in dark suits, and they all behave the same way. The clergy are much the same in the West.

Ironically, the typical Japanese man turns his entire paycheck over to his wife. She gives him his allowance to stay out at night after she has taken what the family needs to live on. The woman completely controls what happens at home, and neither the husband nor the children have much say in her world. To my mind, this is a very strange family arrangement, but it explains a lot about the behavior of the Japanese and their great success in business. Yet it is fueled to a large extent by their absence of fathering at home and their need to find it in the workplace. The reassuring company of other men makes the Japanese business world go 'round!

I shudder to think that our own American society might be headed in the same direction, but already we see signs of it. Business executives ride home to the suburbs late in the evening after their children have gone to bed; they take business trips away from their families for days and weeks at a time. Workingmen stay overtime or work two jobs in order to earn enough money, and the problem for the children is compounded when both parents must or choose to leave the home to work.

To complicate the problem of the absent father, children often learn to perceive their father largely through their mother's eyes, instead of any immediate contact. Without thinking about it, she tells her children what their father is like through the remarks she makes about him when he is not around. Children grow up believing that their father is lazy ("He never does anything around the house."), incompetent ("We'll have to call the repairman."), stupid ("He'll never know."), unsuccessful ("He doesn't make enough money."), uncaring ("He doesn't have the time.") and so on. When he is actually around, they only see the man their mother has described to them, and they never get his immediate energy or life. All too often, he is no more than the absent disciplinarian ("You just wait until your father gets home!").

Even when the portrait painted is not as negative as this, children can never come to really know their father through what their mother tells them about him. Just as a mother's love can never be known by being told about it, so also a father's love can never be known except by experiencing it. And we are talking here about so much more than simply love. What we are talking about is the entire range of masculine qualities and energies that can only be known directly, through experience. When the father is absent, therefore, the masculine can never be truly experienced for what it is. Especially in the case of boys, masculinity must be learned directly. What is learned instead is the masculine *through the filter of the feminine*. I am sure that explains much of the rage in so many boys.

On every "wild man" retreat I have given, I ask the men to discuss in small groups their relationships with their fathers. Without exception, the feedback from the groups always highlights the same two themes: absence and sadness because of that absence.

Not only is the father unable to give a healthy example because of his absence, but even when he is present he usually cannot model religion or spirituality for his children, especially his sons. One priest-friend told me that when he asked men how many could remember their fathers ever praying with them personally, *less than one percent could!* Religion in our culture has become the province of the female, and spirituality has become feminized. American Christianity is much more about belonging and consoling than doing, risking and confronting. Nor can Jesus even provide a real male model for them, for we have become so used to seeing Jesus as God that we never truly see Jesus as a man. He even has blond hair and blue eyes and surely does not have a penis.

In John 10:30 when we hear Jesus saying, "I and the Father are one," we immediately take it in the doctrinal sense that Jesus is identical with God, completely forgetting that the doctrine of the Holy Trinity took three more centuries to formulate and teach. I am not denying that the Son is "of the same substance" (to use the doctrinal terminology) with the Father, but I am pointing out that the Jesus of the Gospels is not yet the "second Person of the Blessed Trinity" but first a "fully human" being who has experienced and trusts his relationship with God. I do not even believe that his human consciousnesss fully knew he was "God," or the whole thing was pretend. Luke says that he "grew" in wisdom, age and grace (2:40). He is a man speaking about his relationship with the God, and calling him *Abba,* Daddy. That is not the operative or common image of Jesus. We were so eager to make him God that we forgot what he came for—to reveal to us what it means to be fully human and still divine!

I usually find that 80 percent of people's operative God image is a combination of their mother and their father images—for good and for ill. If the dad was distant, you will first assume that God is distant; if Mom operated by manipulation, you will assume God does the same and will put up the same defenses; if your family was judgmental, your God will be judgmental, too. Grace, for some dangerous reason, always takes the humble, slow road of building on nature.

The only way out of this vicious circle, of course, is to either have a true inner relationship with God, which will disprove all of the negatives—or to trust everything that Jesus communicated about the nature of God. He is running toward you on the road, losing all his dignity to get at you, even after you have rejected him (Luke 15). He does not even shame you, but throws a party for you, even against the complaints of his other son, your older brother, who is still trapped in tit-for-tat thinking. This story that most of us call the Prodigal Son is one that even the sternest critics think came directly from the teaching of Jesus.

Jesus' God was not just a passionately loving father, but what the English poet, Francis Thompson (1859–1907) would later call a "Hound of Heaven" that chases down the soul "with unhurrying chase, and unperturbed pace." This poem has described Jesus' kind of God for seekers worldwide for over a hundred years. Let's end with just the last few telling verses, and I know it will make you want to read it in its entirety. It has changed many a life, and it illustrates just how much God desires intimacy with each one of us:

> Whom wilt thou find to love ignoble thee,
> Save Me, save only Me?
> All which I took from thee I did but take,
> Not for thy harms,
> But just that thou might'st seek it in My arms.
> All which thy child's mistake
> Fancies as lost, I have stored for thee at home:
> "Rise, clasp my hand, and come!"

It does not get any better than that.

Notes

1. Robert Waldron, *Poetry as Prayer* (Boston: Pauline, 1999). This small book is a prayerful commentary on "The Hound of Heaven," but you can find the poem in many collections of English and religious poetry.

2. Robert Bly, *Iron John* (Reading, Mass: Addison-Wesley, 1990).

SIXTEEN

The Wild Men of India

There are no atheists in India.

—aphorism

I had to go to India to find a culture where both the wild man and the wise man are both understood and appreciated. I am not suggesting that all Indian males necessarily go on the journey I will describe, but I even remember seeing them pictured in a church window in South India. They are part of the cultural heritage and knowledge. Western technology and thinking have made inroads into the traditional Indian culture, and are as everywhere, undermining it, but there is still an idealized template for the whole journey, which is quite different from our concept of getting your information in childhood Sunday School and then "believing" it— usually at that level—for the rest of your life.

Indians understood a man's life in four classic stages. The first stage is that of the student. When a higher-caste boy was in early adolescence, he was historically apprenticed to a guru whose task was to teach the boys in his care what Indian culture and religion teach about life and its mysteries. He teaches them the Indian folkways and the Hindu scriptures, and they learn discipline and self-control through meditation and yoga, which is to say, both mind and body.

The second stage is that of the householder. When a young man is of an age to marry, his parents arrange his wedding and he settles down to raise a family and occupy himself with business. He might become a farmer, a craftsman or a merchant, or even an intellectual, an administrator or a military officer. Today he might even become a professional in the western sense: a doctor, a lawyer, a teacher, an accountant or so on. He is expected not only to provide for his immediate family but also to play a role in his extended family and to contribute to the well-being of his general community in whatever way his time and talents allow. Traditional Indian culture is both family-oriented and civic-minded.

The third stage is that of the seeker. Whereas we tend to take householding and business as the main and even final focus of life, Indians view it as a merely transitional period leading to what we might mistake as early retirement, for it can begin as soon as the man has provided enough for his family that they can get along without him. Generally, this is when his sons are working and providing an income, having themselves become householders, thus freeing him to go on to the next stage in life. Very often it begins around the time that the first grandchildren are born.

The seeker is sometimes referred to as a "forest dweller." Not that all seekers go to live in the woods, but they often do go off to be alone. We might think of them as the Hindu equivalent of monks, even though they join no religious order and go to no monastery. They might even continue to live in the family household, but apart from the others and no longer as the decision-maker. After years of having experienced life, they are now in a position to begin to understand it, to look for the big picture, as it were. They read their scriptures, they meditate and they talk with gurus, seeking to understand the meaning of life.

Compared with this Indian view of life, ours is terribly short-sighted. When we get a job or enter a profession, it is our own material good which we are seeking, or at best the good of our immediate nuclear family. We are not necessarily seeing it as a means of finding our "soul" or discovering the meaning of the larger world. For the East, some of this instinct probably goes back to the life of the Buddha, who disobeying his father's orders, walked outside the doors of his protective palace and discovered the pain of the world. He then resented his father for not telling him about this, and it was the beginning of his conversion. Of course, Jesus was doing a similar thing when he deliberately left his parents at the age of twelve to be "in his Father's house." He never apologized to them for this, even after his mother's correction and worry (Luke 2:41–52). It is, in fact, the only story we have of his youth, and is in many ways classic initiation behavior. The next we hear of him is when he self-initiates at the age of thirty with his forty-day "vision quest" in the desert. Only afterward does he have his role, his occupation, his public manhood, all based in his experience of "beloved sonship."

Our western ideal of old age and retirement is rather individualistic and even hedonistic, although many do go beyond it through service and volunteer work, groups like Elder Hostel, and spiritual retreats and study. But many move away from kids, parents and the community that gave them a living for so many years to some idealized "sun city." You've run in the rat race for so long, maybe you did not really enjoy it, and now at last you have a chance to stretch out, relax and do absolutely nothing. Alternatively, you may see it as a chance to develop your golf swing, to get into that hobby you always wanted, or to fix up the basement now that you have the time to do it yourself. All of these activities are very important, no doubt, but only from one perspective. Nothing in those activities accounts for personal or intellectual growth, concern for others, passing on wisdom or a deeper seeking of God and truth.

But in India, there is still one more stage! The fourth and final stage of the man's spiritual development in India is that of the wise man or holy man. Having sought to comprehend the meaning of life, having moved into the bigger picture, its mysteries reveal themselves to him hopefully in his sixties or seventies. This is what all of life prepared him for. He is now in a position to be sort of a guru himself, not necessarily as a professional teacher, but as a man who can be sought after for wise counsel. He has experienced it all—youth and age, masculinity and femininity, health and sickness, good and evil, society and solitude, trial and failure, feast and famine, activity and silence, life and death—and now he can put it all together in a meaningful whole, both for himself and for anyone who seeks his wisdom.

I must sadly confess that I do not see much understanding of staging in Christianity, even though Jesus himself exemplified much of it, packed into his thirty-some years. By too quickly asserting Jesus' divinity, we have typically avoided what he was exemplifying and teaching us about our humanity. Of course, he did not marry, lived simply, went off to the desert, became a teacher of alternative wisdom, all because he was God, although that does not really follow. Maybe we need to see Jesus as first teaching us how to be human and how to live in this world, instead of just how to "go to heaven." The very word initiation reveals the necessary bias. The concern was about getting *the beginning* right, and then life and eternity would take care of themselves. We have been preoccupied with getting the end right, for some reason. "In case of accident, please call a priest," our Catholic medals said. "Now and at the hour of our death. Amen," we prayed.

Sometimes I wonder if what Jesus meant by a "disciple" (a teachable one) was simply an *adult!* One who had gone through the stages of growing up, letting go, handing over and learning to live out of his or her true self. If you can once in a while get rid of all the pious connotations, you can see that an adult believer is merely one who has stopped hating, blaming, passing on death and negativity. They have become transmitter stations of life. They let everything teach them, even in old age. That is a disciple of Jesus, as far as I am concerned.

Transformative religion is always much more about the *now* than the future.[1] How you do anything is finally how you do everything. How you do relationship is how you do relationship— with your job, your family, animals, nature, the present moment and God. As other teachers have said, "if you are here now, you will be there then." If you can be present to love and life now, you are ready for heaven. If you do not know how to be present, how would you possibly be ready for the Real Presence? If you cannot see the good, the true and the beautiful now, how would you know how to enjoy the "Beatific Vision"? If you cannot allow the beatific embrace of God now, why would you tomorrow when you die? What you are now, what you choose now, what you say yes to now, is what you will be forever.

In my opinion, any culture or religion that teaches you how to live now with attention and caring is preparing you for eternity. Any religion that teaches you to avoid, fear or deny is preparing you for hell, a hell that has already begun.

Note

1. Thomas Keating and Richard Rohr, "The Eternal Now: and how to be there." Recorded conference, 2004 (Center for Action and Contemplation, Box 12464, Albuquerque, NM 87195).

SEVENTEEN

Iron John

Even though the wild man as a masculine archetype has largely disappeared from western culture, we do not have to go back too far in our history to find traces of it. The classic story being used by men's groups today is from *Grimm's Fairy Tales:* the story of Iron John, or *Eisenhans,* as he is called in German. I have summarized the story below.

* * *

Once upon a time there lived a king whose castle was right next to a large forest where all sorts of game roamed about. One day he sent a royal hunter into the forest to shoot a deer, but the hunter did not return. "Perhaps he had an accident," thought the king, so the very next day he sent two other hunters into the forest to look for the one who was missing, but they did not come back, either. On the third day he gathered all the royal hunters together and instructed them, "Search the entire forest and do not return until you have found the three missing men." But all these hunters, too, like the first three, never came back. Even the hunting dogs they had taken into the forest were never seen again.

From that day forward, no one dared venture into the forest nor did they see anything moving except for an occasional eagle or hawk flying above. The forest lay completely still and silent.

This state of affairs went on for years, until one day a hunter from a distant land asked the king if he could look for game in the royal forest. Remembering what had happened to the missing men, the king was reluctant to grant the request. He told the hunter, "I am very afraid that if you went into the dangerous forest you would fare no better than the others, and that you would never get out of it alive." To which the hunter replied, "My lord, I do not know the meaning of fear. I will gladly face the danger."

Into the forest strode the hunter with his hound. It was not long before the dog picked up the scent of a deer and barked for the hunter to follow him. Then the dog ran ahead, until he came to the edge of a pool of water that was so deep he hesitated before trying to cross it. Suddenly, a bare arm reached up out of the dark pond, grabbed the hound and pulled him under.

When the hunter saw what had happened, he ran back to the castle and got three men with buckets to empty all the water out of the pond. They worked hard for many hours, and as the dark waters began to be drained away, they beheld a wild man lying on the bottom. His body was covered with hair the color of rusted iron. The hunter and his helpers bound the wild man with ropes and dragged him off to the castle.

The sight of the wild man caused great wonder and alarm, so the king had him locked in an iron cage in the middle of the courtyard. He forbade anyone under threat of exile to open the door to the cage, and he entrusted the key to no one less than the queen herself. And from then on, anyone could again go safely into the forest.

Now, the king had a son who was eight years old, and one day when the prince was playing in the courtyard with his golden ball, the ball bounced into the iron cage. "Give me back my ball," said the boy. "Not until you open the door for me," answered the wild man. "No," said the boy, "I dare not do that. The king has forbidden it." And with that, he ran away.

The very next day, however, the boy came back and demanded his ball again. Again the wild man said, "Open the door for me." But the boy would not do it.

On the third day, the king went off on a hunt. His son came back yet again, and this time he said, "Even if I wanted to, I could not open the door because I do not have the key." To which the wild man replied, "It is lying under your mother's pillow. You can surely get it." Upon hearing this, the boy threw all care to the wind, for he really wanted his ball, and stole the key.

The young prince returned shortly and unfastened the lock, but as he pulled the heavy door open, it pinched his finger. As soon as the door swung open, the wild man stepped out, gave the boy his golden ball and started to hurry away. But the boy was frightened, and he called after him, "Oh, wild man, if you run away I shall be punished! Please don't run away!" Whereupon the wild man turned around and came back. He picked the boy up, sat him on his shoulders and carried him off into the forest.

* * *

What are we to make of this tale? Like so many other fables and myths it is really an allegory with a great deal of meaning hidden in it. It is exactly the type of story that depth psychologists frequently analyze by taking the characters and their actions as symbols of what is going on inside a person even though the person may be completely unaware of it. In this particular case, however, the story is not someone's personal dream but a cultural myth that represents something in what Carl Jung and others have called the collective unconscious. From that perspective, it is clearly a tale about the wild man in all of us.

Let us examine the symbolism step-by-step.[1]

At the outset, the king's hunters disappear without a trace. Although he sends others out to look for them, the king never asks the one question that really needs to be asked, namely, what is it that is causing the men to be lost? Like most of us, the king turns away from his problem rather than facing it. In this instance, the problem obviously has something to do with the loss of manpower or manliness. He leaves the forest, which is the part of his life with the problem in it, undisturbed. All appears to be peaceful and quiet, but the danger in fact has not gone away.

The only one with the courage to face the danger is a foreigner who discovers where the cause of the king's problem is hidden. He calls for assistance, and with great labor he and the others empty out the water from the deep pond. The stranger represents a certain willingness to look into the problem area, but the king himself at the same time represents continued resistance to the idea. The men with buckets dip into the dark pool of the unconscious, but it is only with great effort that they uncover this mysterious region in order to get to the bottom of things.

What they find is a big, hairy, naked man. They tie him up and bring him back to the castle, where the people are fascinated by the wild man's brute energy. The king does not know what to do with this uncontrolled and frightening strength, however, so he locks the wild man up where he can do no harm. With that, the king returns to his old pursuits, as though nothing at all has happened. Very symbolically, though, the queen holds the key to the wild man's cage, for the woman has the power to unlock his energy or, as in this case, to keep it locked up.

Next on the scene comes the young prince. He is eight years old, what used to be called the "age of reason," when children emerge from unreflective innocence and begin thinking. He is also playing with a golden ball, which in mythology often represents wholeness. So the boy in his innocence comes face-to-face with his father's wild man who, because the boy is the king's son, is also his own wild man. The boy wants his wholeness, but the only way he can get it is to let the wild man out.

Iron John tells him that the key to it all is under the queen's pillow for, as we have seen, the way to the wild man is through a proper relationship with the feminine, not too far and not too close. The boy is afraid of what might happen to him if he lets out the wild man, but his desire for wholeness prompts him to sneak into his mother's bedroom anyway to steal the key.

What are we to make of this? I myself take it to symbolize the ambiguity of the feminine in most of our lives. On the one hand, the wild man locked inside us is telling us that his incredible strength can be reached by moving into the space of the feminine, yet so often the woman who could lead us into that space wants to prevent us from getting in touch with the wild man. Rebekah so feared her hairy, hunter son, Esau, that she betrayed him in favor of the gentle Jacob (see Genesis 27). This is not a new issue.

In my own life, I have to admit, that woman is my mother. Right from the very beginning of my ministry, whenever my mother would hear about me getting into strange things like charismatic Masses or war protests, she would call me up and chide me for trying to be different. Why can't I just be the nice, docile priest she had wanted her son to be, she always wants to know. It is very hard to resist those maternal voices that do not understand or support risk taking.

I often see the same in other priests' lives, not just in reference to their mothers but in reference to "our holy mother, the church," as we used to say. Holy mother doesn't want her sons to be different; she does not want them to do anything that might rock the boat or tarnish the family image, even if they are doing it to promote the gospel, which is what the church is supposed to be all about. In most male puberty rites the young boy must separate from his mother. If you think this is strange or unnecessary, witness Jesus' action at age twelve in the temple (Luke 2:41–52).

We can imagine the boy's trepidation as he returns from the queen's bedroom with the key. Will the wild man eat him? Will he be punished by his well-meaning but possessive parents? Overcoming his doubts, the boy swings open the heavy door, suffering a small hurt as he does this. The wild man never emerges without pain, yet it is never as great as we might have feared.

Once the wild man is let out, he is surprisingly gentle. He does not devour the boy and he gives him back his ball, as he had promised. Then, when the wild man begins to run off, the boy begins to fear his parents again, so the wild man returns and carries the boy off on his shoulders.

In the final scene, the boy—the innocent, inquiring yet brave boy in each of us—has befriended the wild man, whose mighty energy now carries him off. To where? The forest. But what lies in the forest? The tale ends ambiguously.

Should we think that the boy becomes a wild man like Iron John, lurking in a muddy pool to devour unwary passersby? I prefer to think that the pair, now united, are different from what each of them was separately. The boy seated on his shoulders has become the wild man's eyes and vision, and the wild man has become the boy's masculine energy—the energy his father never gave him.

Together they go off to adventure in the forest—and probably beyond.

It is genuinely a great and telling story, that surely proceeded from our human depths, and our male desire. I can see why Robert Bly almost launched the whole secular men's movement by just telling this one story, and telling it well.

Note

1. Bly, *Iron John*.

EIGHTEEN

Confronts and Retreats

Retreats are a good thing. It's good to get away from it all, to find some quiet time, to seek God, ourselves and the truth of things. We need that time away from the demands and distractions of our daily routine, so we can get into that space where we can just be, reflect and contemplate. If we never make a retreat, we may never find our center. It seems we need to regularly withdraw from business as usual, all our roles and usual payoffs, to see things clearly. Retreats are good for letting go of the shallow self and moving into the deeper self.

For some people, however, making retreats and taking vacations has become a way of life. But one is never sure what exactly it is that they are getting away from and what they are going toward. When the world gets to be too much for them, they make a retreat, which is not a bad idea. When their friends are going, they go on a retreat. When a new spiritual director comes to town, they are anxious to hear what she or he has to offer. When they have nothing else to do, they make another retreat. They feel good about it. It feels like a regular oil change, but no new engine is really apparent. It is often informational or a little cosmetic surgery, but seldom transformational—not back to their true self in God, not back to "the face they had before they were born."

Having seen folks like this come and go time after time, some spiritual directors I know have made a rule that the only people they will work with are those who are engaged in some form of service or volunteer work for others. They have come to the conclusion that *those who never stretch between retreats never stretch during retreats.* In the name of searching for God, such would-be retreatants were often really running away from God. They were into religion, churchy things and pious practices, but they really weren't into the path itself. Some retreat masters don't want to support any addiction to navel gazing, camouflage and avoidance of the real issues. Piety is a great cover very often.

I think a better rule would be that for every retreat in your life, there should also be at least one "confront." There should be something you've come up against, something you've wrestled with, something you've tried to do in the world. If you've confronted some hardness in society, some evil in the world, some intransigence in the church, then you have a reason to retreat and gather your inner strength. A lot of spiritual energy is stored in several unique places: loneliness, silence and fear. You can find that energy by going there and staying there.

Thomas Merton once told the assembled Cistercian abbots that they should stop accepting any candidates for the monastery who had not weathered at least one spiritual crisis, and come out positive and hopeful. In fact, he felt it was so important in this age of protecting young people from all crises, that he even suggested the abbots "manufacture" a spiritual crisis for any incoming novice, and see how he deals with it—before they accept him! Genius. That is probably what the old stories of shocking or scandalizing the candidate were about, or leaving him unattended on the doorstep for several days. What can we hope for now when we actually pay their airfare to come and visit the monastery? All comfortable "retreats" without any testing in the reality world of "confronts." It is a set-up for spiritual mediocrity and even phoniness.

I would say that if you only think about Jesus, "believe" Jesus and believe things about Jesus, not much new is going to happen. It is the risk of "acting" like Jesus acted that reconfigures your soul. We are converted by new circumstances much more than by new ideas. Or as I like to say, *we do not think ourselves into new ways of living, we live ourselves into new ways of thinking.* To know and not to act is not to know. Reality and circumstances, unavoidable circumstances, are normally what convert us. Reality is the greatest ally of God. It is the things you cannot do anything with—the useless things—and the things you cannot do anything about—the necessary things—that tend to do something with you!

In my own life I have given hundreds of retreats and thousands of sermons. I know that when I talk, people sometimes get new ideas and they sometimes even get inspired. But they don't often get converted, they aren't really changed. It takes more than words to do that. What converts people are real-life situations. What changes people are confrontations, looking at something they don't want to deal with straight in the face, or looking at life from a new vantage point. Observe your point from an honest perspective. Change your viewpoint every now and then, and stand in another pair of shoes looking back at yourself. How else will you ever get free? It is essential for human empathy. It is necessary, or we remain largely narcissistic and trapped in our own ego and culture. This is probably the core meaning of religious pilgrimage, which requires that you leave home.

When I established the Center for Action and Contemplation in New Mexico in 1987, well-meaning folks asked if I had not put the words in the wrong order. Shouldn't "contemplation" come first, they asked. No, it was deliberate, I told them. We have nothing to contemplate—until we have acted and moved beyond ourselves, and outside of our comfort zone. We will see everything through mere self-interest. It is a dance, however, a divine two-step, back and forth between action and contemplation. It is an art form that takes your whole life to perfect, till eventually you are busily *acting* with full-conscious union with God, and you are *contemplating* while holding, carrying and transforming the pain of the world within you.

For much of our Catholic lives we were warned to avoid the near occasions of sin. Perhaps we should think instead of "near occasions of grace." We need to put ourselves in situations where we are forced to do a certain about-face. That's what conversion basically means: turning around. At the very least, we need to move out of our "over-developed world" and confront the dark underworld of poverty on which it floats. We need to see, not just how the other half lives, but how the other 90 percent of the people in the world are forced to live.

Every viewpoint is a view from a point. And your view depends on the point where you stand. If you stand at the top of the heap, you can't see, feel or experience life the way it is at the bottom. The people at the top can afford to be conservative. They've made it, so they really have no felt need for change or reform. They don't feel the pinch. They have the power, so they use it to preserve and defend. They have the leisure, so they can dabble in religion and go on retreats.

The people at the bottom don't have the luxury of being conservative. They have to push for change. They have to make new things happen. They have to confront the reality that they've been handed—the dead-end jobs, the run-down housing, the crime in the streets, the drugs in the schools—and face it head-on. If they are not to be crushed by it, they have to fight it. They have to struggle for liberation. But of course, you can also be trapped at the bottom—in bitterness, greed and anger. Even the poor man must make an effort to stand in the position of responsibility and authority, or there is something that he does not understand either. There is no structural position that is naturally enlightened. All things being equal, *the view from the side of suffering is the privileged position of the Gospel,*[1] but sometimes people at the top have learned from suffering more than those at the bottom, who only fight it.

We do not convert ourselves. We are all converted—by the push and tug of the real—and usually in spite of ourselves. God does it. We allow it.

Note

1. Richard Rohr, "The Bias from the Bottom." Recorded conference (Center for Action and Contemplation, Box 12464, Albuquerque, NM 87195).

NINETEEN

Male Sexuality and the Love of God

"I was afraid because I was naked, so I hid," said Adam.
"Who told you that you were naked?" Yahweh said in return.
—GENESIS 3:9–10

Recently, a young woman told me that she was breaking up with her boyfriend, and when I asked her why, she said it was because he never did anything on his own. He never took the initiative, either in their relationship or in the rest of his life. He was always a follower, never a doer, never proactive about anything. She was the one who always had to suggest things to do and places to go. He was always attentive and caring, considerate and cooperative, but he never came up with a new idea and asked her to come along. Slowly she lost respect for him as a man, and in the end, she pitied him. He had no male energy to challenge and energize her own energy.

I know a number of women who pity their husbands. They cannot admire them because they never do anything to arouse their wives' admiration. The men go to work and come home dutifully every day. They take out the garbage and do whatever the wives ask them to do, but that's the extent of their energy. I have no idea how the men are in bed, but I suspect they don't surprise their wives there either. Perhaps the men's initiative has been beaten down or driven out of them, but it's not there. So the wives love them, but they do not respect them, and there is probably a disappointment in their children, too. Sons especially want their dads to take them into new, different and challenging worlds, not just build picket fences around them.

Some believe, as I do too, that biology is also destiny. Our meaning is partly encoded in our body, our genes, our shape and physicality. Nowhere is this more true than in our sexuality. How we love is finally who we are. Archetypally for men, it has something to do with both carrying and planting seeds. For women, it means receiving, protecting and nurturing what is planted. I know some will not agree with me here, particularly some branches of feminism, but I ask you to indulge me.

I am not saying that men have no need to nurture what they have created, nor that women haven't any ability to create or plant seeds. But I believe that there is a biological urgency and a primal understanding from what is written in our bodies as men and women. For me, it is just the principle of the incarnation. The Word has become our flesh too, and that flesh longs to express itself in other words. The deepest inscription in the masculine soul is to generate life in others. It is probably why sexual intercourse is such a strong and relentless need in the male. He is not oversexed, but it is the way that God coded him for relationship and encounter. Otherwise, many men would remain loners and self-sufficient. Let's be honest, every man is proud of his erect penis, but perhaps, strange as it sounds, he should meditate on it and see what it is telling him about his deeper nature. Let's for a moment look at our male genitalia as a metaphor for manhood. Don't be afraid like Adam was.

The male penis is, first of all, both soft and hard. That is its first message. There is a proper place for both in our lives, vulnerability and strength, letting go and firmness. Wisdom is to know when, where and how. The male penis is not a weapon or a mere tool, but it is a means of making contact, literally "reaching out" for the other, not to hurt or invade, but to pleasure and delight—mutually! It is the seed planter, the life giver, the enjoyer and the enjoyed. Not just me, and not just the other, but both simultaneously. Is that not an ideal metaphor for what all human relationships should be? And maybe even what morality should be. I bet you never imagined you could learn that from your male body.

John Duns Scotus, who I mentioned earlier, taught that the perfection of a moral act was not to be found by pushing it as far as possible on the "selfless" scale (which is the form of morality that has largely formed the West, and almost everybody reacts against, because it is impossible 99.9 percent of the time). With his usual subtle wisdom, which is why the church named him "The Subtle Doctor," he says that the perfection of a moral act is to find the proper balance between the focus inward and the focus outward, which he calls the "two natural affections" or metaphysical desires.[1] Satan's fall he taught, was not merely self-love, a certain degree of which is required and necessary, but *disordered self-love!* How different the history of Christian morality could have been, if we had only been taught this. It is balancing love of self with love of the other that makes for moral integrity, just as in true love making. It is holding my own boundaries, while also going beyond them for the sake of the other. Good stuff, that even simple people can understand and profit from.

The issue, as the East and most Native religions have always intuited, is to seek *harmony and balance* instead of mere obligation and moral requirement. Most people would be willing to try that, whereas this "total selflessness" ideal only backfires and ends up ironically making many Christians actually quite selfish. Basically, they give up on the gospel, thinking it is asking them to be martyrs every minute. Here I am applying the same to sexuality. What a different and humanizing starting point that would have been, instead of something as limited and legalistic as the starting point most of us were given: "every act of sexual pleasure outside of heterosexual acts open to procreation are sinful." That negative approach has not brought many people, if any, closer to the love of God. "No" of itself is not wisdom. It is no more than a first-stage boundary marking. It is a container to get you in the right struggle, but it is not the contents.

But let's go even further, because masculine energy is not just phallic but also scrotal. That most vulnerable, tender and protected part of a man—his testicles—are an essential symbol of his power and his possibility. He carries a quiet, hidden seed, in fact billions of them (what does that in itself say?), but he also has a capacity for containment and protection of them, just like the female has in her placenta and womb. His scrotum is a place of patient ripening, a place of dark, wet mystery, that must be protected and kept warm. It becomes power and pleasure when it comes forth. The male "birth canal," however, is largely associated with pleasure, whereas the female birth canal both enjoys pleasure and suffers the great pain of labor. This is perhaps why many deemed it necessary for the man to bleed and suffer pain in his penis during initiation. He needed to be taught the inherent connection between pain and new life. Thus the emergence in two-thirds of the cultures of the world of something the West no longer understands—male circumcision as a sacred wounding, leading to wisdom and even "covenant" with God![2]

An exaggerated phallic energy, uninformed by scrotal energy, is usually a sign of an intrusive, domineering and exploitive male. In other words, your strong phallus must always remember that it carries a soft sac of tenderness right beneath. The hard man without any softness is dangerous. It is macho overcompensation rather than true masculine self-confidence. The drivenness of the businessman, the sterility of the academic, the rigidity of the believer, the war games of the military, the stabbing finger of the opinionated, the punishing inner father—these are all indications of the phallic man, not the true wise man, who is always both hard and soft—and often at the same time. The so-called "fist in a velvet glove" might not be a bad metaphor for the penis.

Theologically speaking, masculine energy is the energy of God the creator. Maybe that is why both the Hebrew and Christian traditions tended to image God as Father. They preserved the Mother image for nurturance, sustenance and enjoyment. When we experience ourselves as givers of life, we know God the Father—not conceptually but experientially. Our giving spirit is the Father's creative spirit moving through us. When it flows, we allow it to flow, and consciously know it is the very life of God flowing through us, we call it the Holy Spirit. We replicate the Trinity, as women do too, but in a different way perhaps. I *am* the Body of Christ, I carry the image of the Creator himself, and their shared life flows through me as the Holy Spirit. As John 7:39 says, "from the believer's breast shall flow fountains of living water." A full man or woman are living icons of the Trinitarian life.[3]

This desire to be a source of creation is a man's deepest identification with God the Father. It expresses itself in the desire for some form of fatherhood, whether it be to have children in the usual physical sense or to have spiritual children in the sense of fostering growth and maturity in others, or just to tend the crops, the earth and suffering humanity. My desire to speak and to write in order to give birth to something new in the lives of others, for example, expresses my own deepest need to be a father, to be an author of new life. When you actually "author" life in others, you have authority, whether you have any titles or degrees or not. In fact, I am not sure real authority comes in any other way.

A Jewish rabbi once made much the same point in speaking about prayer. "When I pray," he said, "I *am* God." That's a bold and unorthodox way to put it, but it is the same daring we see in Jesus when his opponents get upset with him for claiming that he is a son of God, and he says back to them, "Is it not written in your own law:

'you too are gods'...and Scripture cannot be rejected" (John 10:34–35). That is the consistent, scary language of mystical religion, in other words, religion based on inner experience and "knowing" for yourself, and not just religion based on "believing" what other people tell you or, even worse, believing things that are hard to believe (as if that would somehow please God!). We need men who know, know for themselves, and mostly who know who they are.[4] We need mystical religion and not just requirement religion. Men will not be satisfied with any religion that gives them anything less than their Divine Sonship, nor should they be.

At our baptism we were told that we are sons of God, but most of us do not really believe it. We still keep trying to merit God's love, as if we could.[5] It also tends to make us self-preoccupied instead of in love with God. We think we have to be good and earn the Father's approval, even though God's total love and offer of Divine intimacy has already been given to us. Our holiness is inherent, discovered and recognized, not earned or attained by any kind of behavior. We are the "dwelling place of the Holy Spirit" (2 Corinthians 2:22) according to Paul, and "sharers in the divine nature" (2 Peter 1:4) according to Peter.

We do not have to become sons of God; we *are* sons of God. What was once interior to God, within the Trinity, is now flowing through us. The mystery of the Trinity is ours by grace, free gift and invitation. Jesus moved into space and time to assure us that we were invited into the eternal and divine Dance. We are called "adopted sons" by Saint Paul, but we are sons of God nevertheless. We do not need to spend our efforts trying to earn what we already have.

But I am further convinced that this power is written into our very body structure, even that generative and genital part from which all generation flows, that very part which we are most proud of and most ashamed of at the same time. "Who told you that you were naked?" Yahweh says to Adam at the very beginning of creation (Genesis 3:9–10), as if to say, "I created you that way, why are you afraid of it?" Silly and scandalous as it will sound to some of you, our penises and testicles themselves, our generative functions, are a metaphor for our Divine destiny. The Jewish people were not as prudish as most Christians are about such things, and the Jewish people saw the marking of the penis as the very act that made you a "son of the covenant" with God. It was a public "sacrament." They were not primitive or obscene people but people who knew how to read the primal symbols correctly. For some strange reason, it is the things right in front of us (or in this case, directly south) that remain most hidden in their meanings.

Allow me to end this chapter with a quote from T.S. Eliot's "Choruses from the Rock," where as usual, he sums it up in terse and select words:

> The Lord who created must wish us to create,
> And employ our creation again in his service,
> Which is already his service in creating,
> For man is joined spirit and body,
> And therefore must serve as spirit and body.
> Visible and invisible, two worlds meet in Man;
> Visible and invisible must meet in his Temple;
> You must not deny the body.

Notes

1. Ingham, *Scotus for Dunces,* p. 87ff.

2. David Gollaher, *Circumcision: A History of the World's Most Controversial Surgery* (New York: Basic Books, 2000).

3. Rohr, "The Divine Dance."

4. Rohr, "True Self/False Self."

5. Philip Gulley and James Mulholland, *If Grace is True: Why God Will Save Every Person* (San Francisco: Harper, 2003).

TWENTY

God as Paradox:
Powerful Powerlessness

A striking portrayal of the father-son relationship I have been describing hangs in a most unlikely place—although it's not that unlikely when you consider the Christian belief in the Trinity. I came across it in the Cistercian monastery of Heilsbronner Müenster in Germany, where it hangs above the Marian altar. The painting impressed me so profoundly that I bought a copy of it for my study, and every time I looked at it I saw more and more in it. The insight of its painter, Sebastian Dayg, an almost unknown artist of the early sixteenth century, into the relationship between the Father and the Son still impresses me.

Look at the stereotypical figure of God the Father. He's a stern old man with a flowing gray beard, and in his left hand he holds the orb that in medieval times symbolized kingly power. If you look more closely, though, you see that the orb of power is slipping from his hand! God the Father, the supreme authority figure, is supposedly in control of the whole world, and yet he seems to be losing that control. Maybe he is sure enough of his own power that he can let go of it. He is so certain of his own authority that he doesn't have to manipulate or dominate. He is self-possessed enough that he can allow for freedom, error and weakness.

At the same time that the Father allows us our freedom, he is also demanding. This is symbolized in the painting by a large sword that the Father holds in his right hand, wielding it over his head. This is the expectant and exacting side of God, summoning us to use well the freedom he has given us and challenging us to be all that we can be. In human fathers it's a kind of love that pushes and won't put up with excuses. It's a very masculine, tough love, not brutal or threatening, just hopeful and effective. That's a very modern concept, but this artist saw it in God almost five centuries ago.

The other side of God in the picture is the Son. In the painting this is symbolized by Jesus, stripped almost naked and still wearing the crown of thorns. If the Father is the strong and demanding side of God, the Son is the weak and suffering side, the part of God that identifies with our brokenness and even with our sinfulness. God asks a lot of us, but God also knows our feebleness and limitations by solidarity with us. In the painting the Father is looking into the

Son's eyes and the Son is looking into the Father's eyes in perfect reciprocity and mutual understanding. Strength is honoring weakness and weakness is honoring strength. They know they need one another.

As if to emphasize his human weakness, Jesus' right thumb is in the bleeding wound in his side and his fingers pointing toward it, but his left hand reaches up and grabs the sword that is poised above the head of these two figures. The Son holds back the sternness of the Father and prevents it from being too severe, so that *the toughness and tenderness of God are in perfect balance.* We addressed many official prayers with the phrase "Almighty and Merciful God," and the intuition was right, but it seems the way that God is almighty in precisely in being merciful! Symbolizing this balance, the sword itself is perfectly horizontal. If the Father is the powerful side of God, the Son is the vulnerable side. The two are in perfect tension, the Father in this painting representing the powerlessness of divine power and the Son representing the power of divine powerlessness. The creative energy that tension releases is symbolized by the dove of the Holy Spirit, which, appropriately enough, hovers on the balanced sword. It is this same kind of creative energy that is released whenever strength and gentleness understand and respect each other. It sounds lovely and poetic, but be honest, it is not the general pattern. Most of us are one or the other, and seldom strike the balance of sword and spirit.

But that's only half the picture. In this painting the Trinity are off to the left side, and across the space in the middle stands a woman. She is Mary who, in medieval art, symbolizes the whole church because in relation to the constant Divine Initiative, humanity is receptively feminine. We, like her, must say, "let it be" to the Divine Indwelling. Her eyes gaze not at any one of the Trinity but toward the space at their center, as if contemplating the whole mystery. A faint smile suggests she is admiring and respecting what she beholds, letting God be God. Yet her right hand is touching her breast, as if to indicate she knows that God was and still is within her. She protects that identity.

Mary is dressed in a long gown and a flowing cape, and with her left hand she is holding up the cape to shield the figures standing behind her. Those figures are all men of power, prelates bedecked in vestments and tiaras and miters and kings with their crowns and symbols of authority. Unlike the woman, these men are not looking at the Trinity. They are gazing in every other direction but God, which tells me that the artist knew that men of power get so caught up in their roles and status that they lose sight of God. So in one sense Mary is protecting them from the Father's sword, but in another she is telling them that they are not ready for the mystery of God's both tough and tender love. Only one joins the Eternal Feminine in her gaze, the one with bowed head and folded hands. Only the centered and humble man joins her in recognition and delight in the divine paradox.

After reflecting on this wonderful painting for many years now, I honestly wonder how comfortable Christianity is with its Christ. Did he just happen to be the available God figure for the West, but we don't really care much about his message? We are clearly much more concerned with worshiping him than following him, which is all he asked us to do. This wounded half of God, this "lamb" of a God, must be an embarrassment and a serious threat to us, if we would be honest. But fortunately, Mary, image of the true church, is ready, smiling and waiting to offer her next "Let it Be." She is ready to let God be God, God be mystery, God be paradox and even to let God be free.

Humanity stands behind her left arm, waiting to see and accept and love the same.

TWENTY-ONE

Spiritual Fathering, Male Mothering

If you love tenderly your brother according to the flesh, how much more should you not love your brother in the Spirit.

—SAINT FRANCIS OF ASSISI to his followers

Since our wholeness is not always given to us by our natural fathers, we often have to receive it elsewhere. We need partners on the journey, mentors along the path. We need the bonding of what I am going to call "male mothers." Lest you think that is unneeded or strange, note many men's intense loyalty and love toward a good boss or teacher, like Forrest Gump's "Sergeant Dan," or the student adoration of "Mr. Chips" or Robin Williams in *Dead Poet's Society,* or even Rumi's ecstatic love of his spiritual guide, Shams.

Any man who protects, values and instructs a younger man in how to survive and succeed is his male mother. We need a man to be in solidarity with us, so that we can learn what it means to be in solidarity *with ourselves,* and eventually with others in the same way. Oriental religions take this as normative, but it largely became an "ordained office" in the West, more than real spiritual direction or the practical guidance of souls or the master/student relationship we see in Islam, Hinduism, Buddhism and Confucianism.

Interestingly enough, the biological father is hardly ever the initiator of his own son. There is too much tension in the relationship. For one thing, they are both in love with the same woman. Older and unrelated males are almost always the initiators of the boy into manhood. Often it is a man that the boy seeks out on his own. The mother leads the son through boyhood, but other men must "kill the boy softly" and "save Private Ryan" so that the man can emerge. We have no rite, expectation or easy possibility of this in our culture. We *must* learn how. M.A.L.Es (Men as Learners and Elders) has taken it as its task to reintroduce this possibility in our culture "within five generations." We owe it to ourselves and future generations, although for now we are just trying to create a critical mass of adult-initiated men.

Eastern religions, the desert fathers and Eastern Orthodox Christianity are much more aware of this need than we in the western church have been. They are much more relational than merely informational. When the time comes for a boy in the East to take his spiritual development seriously, he is given a mentor, a master, a guru—not so much that he can learn facts or doctrines from him but so that he can pick up the energy of his teacher by observation and by personal identification with him. The closest we have is the occasional father confessor or the spiritual director. Protestantism hardly has it at all, since they transferred much of the spiritual journey to the moral and informational level instead of the mystical.

It is strange how we have forgotten how Jesus formed his disciples. We can read all the words of Jesus in the Gospels in a matter of hours, but Jesus spent three long years discipling the men who followed him. What he gave them was not so much his words but his example and his energy, his time and his touch. "Where do you live?" said the first two disciples of Jesus. "Come and see," he replied, "so they went and saw where he lived, and stayed with him the rest of that day" (John 1:39). What a telling account, and not surprisingly from John's Gospel, the beloved disciple, who had even laid his head on the breast of Jesus—an act that would be unthinkable in most homophobic cultures today. They knew how energy was passed, and it was not primarily by sermons and books, but by relationships and presence.

Whether we are conscious of it or not, we do draw on other people's spirit. We might describe it as a personality to which we are attracted or from which we are repelled. We might say we like a person's character or are turned off by his or her temperament. Very often it is not so much that we react to what is said, but rather to the energy with which things are said and done. Two people can hold the same opinion, but we feel invited to accept it when one of them presents it, and we feel cold and unmoved when we hear it from the other. It's not the idea that we hear, as much as the positive or negative energy behind it.

Any father knows that he can tell his three year old a big thing in a calm voice, and a little thing in an excited voice, and the child will always respond to the excited voice. One young father told me recently that he forgot to get his usual gift after being away from home for a few days in Cleveland, so he picked up a simple bag of gummy bears at the airport and in a thrilled voice told his boy, "These are special gummy bears all the way from Cleveland, Ohio!" The boy was overjoyed and soon bragged to his friends about his "gummy bears from Cleveland"! His dad's excitement made it exciting, not really the gift.

A priest, to whom I was a sort of spiritual father, came to see me once. Some people in his parish were constantly objecting to many of the things he did, pointing out when he did not follow the rubrics for the liturgy exactly, protesting when he talked about social concerns in his sermons, complaining that he did not put enough emphasis on Catholic doctrine, threatening to write to the bishop and so on. He was being bombarded by negative energy and at a certain point it began to get to him. He was losing the enthusiasm he had brought to that parish, he was beginning to feel anger and fear infecting his ministry, he was doubting his gifts as a priest and his abilities as a man.

First and foremost, this priest needed someone to just listen to him, to allow him to express his fears and frustrations, his anger and self-doubt. He also needed some reassurance from someone who had walked the journey ahead of him that what he was experiencing was normal and that it was possible to deal with it. He was needing to hear from someone like a grandfather, someone who had been there before and who could assure him that he was not crazy. He needed to "feel" from another man's experience what boundaries were worth protecting and what boundaries didn't really matter. I hope I was able to do that for him, but I didn't give him any "answers" at all. I just listened, easily cared and hopefully received him. He left feeling "wonderful!", which even surprised me, because I thought I had given him next to nothing. A little bit goes a long way when the other person is ready and willing to believe it and receive it. He did.

The eastern religious traditions, as I said above, make more provision for this need than our own does. After I had given a retreat in Nepal in the 1970s, I was given the opportunity to meet a Hindu guru, a spiritual teacher or wise man. As soon as I entered his small house, almost like a hermitage, on the outskirts of Katmandu, I was aware of being in the presence of something I could only call grandfather energy. When I talked with him, I had the impression that he knew ahead of time everything I was bringing up. He had walked the journey ahead of me, and he was far more advanced in the spiritual life than I was, so he simply recognized the confusions I brought to him, and he confirmed many of the insights I had about spiritual growth. He actually "held" me more than he talked to me. (This happened to me again in Kerala, South India, in 2003, with a Catholic guru who "read my soul" and told me things about me that he had no way of knowing by natural means. It surely breaks down our scientific model of how knowledge is acquired.)

While we talked, I noticed a picture of his own teacher, the guru who had been a spiritual father and grandfather to him. Whenever he mentioned his teacher, his eyes brightened with excitement. At one point he explained to me that the entire Hindu tradition of spirituality was built on a father-son relationship. As if to remind the pupil of the importance of this relationship, tradition requires that whenever he comes into the presence of his guru, he should kneel and bow down, saying, "May I be so humble before you, my spiritual father, that even the dust can crush me." A very poetic greeting, to be sure, but it makes space for an immense trust relationship that allows power and energy to pass from one man to another.

On another occasion I was talking with Jim Wallis, the pastor of the Sojourners community in Washington, D.C. Jim and I have a lot in common since we are about the same age, we are both founders of communities, and we have experienced many of the same ups and downs in our ministries during the years. Jim made the observation that one of the hardest things about being in our position is that there are no father figures around for us. There are very few men who have founded and pastored alternative Christian communities and who have already been through what we're going through (Clarence Jordan of Koinonia in Georgia, Gordon Cosby of the Church of the Saviour in Washington and Jean Vanier of L'Arche being the only ones we could originally think of). We found ourselves in the first generation of a church that was very different from the way the church had been for centuries. The usual rules of parish life don't apply to us in many cases, and we find ourselves having to invent an entirely new set of rules, learning by trial and error. Sometimes, we admitted, we would both like to be able to let it all hang out in front of someone who could just sit there and listen calmly while we were panicking. We have done the best we could by "brothering" one another along the way for over thirty years now, but we both longed for a male mother.

I'm sure that this is equally true of men in the business world or any world. We all need someone with inner authority who can let us know we are OK, that what we are going through is normal, and what battles are worth fighting. Sometimes we just need to hear from someone who believes in us, but who believes in us enough also to challenge us. Strangely, in their presence, the assurance and self-confidence are there, almost by magic, and almost embarrassingly so. It is humbling and wonderful to be a spiritual son. But friendship, even basic male friendship, is really not that common among men. We are afraid to go there, but even worse, it is not often available or offered.

I have no doubt that one of the main reasons I have done some interesting things in my life is that I have known a number of men who believed in me throughout my formation. I remember one older friar who told me as a young Franciscan, "Richard, I want you always to trust your intuitions. Promise me that you will always trust them, even if they are wrong once in a while. The direction is right and I will personally fight for you in the background if it ever comes to that." Need I say more? He was God for me at that point. He was my spiritual father on that day. And one spiritual father, or brother, can make up for a hundred negative ones.

TWENTY-TWO

The Young Boy
and the Old Man

When Elijah returns "He will turn the hearts of fathers to
their children, and the hearts of children to their fathers."
—MALACHI 3:24, the very last words of the Old Testament

Depth psychology, which in some respects is a modern secular
version of traditional spirituality and deals with many of the same
issues, tells us that our lives are often guided by subconscious
images called archetypes. Carl Jung claims that some of these
archetypes are so basic to our lives as human beings they are
found in peoples all over the world. These fundamental patterns
show up in dreams and behavior in every culture, and they appear
in symbols and stories that go as far back in time as we want to go.

Two of the more fundamental archetypes underlying male
consciousness are the young boy and the old man, the inner child
and the inner grandfather. They are found in each of us to varying
degrees, and in our life cycle we hope to journey from one to the
other. Some men, unfortunately, over identify with one archetype
and, hence, become compulsive and unbalanced personalities.
Interestingly, though, as we head toward the end of the journey,
the two normally are integrated, and in our old age we are able to
complete the circle and regain much of the freshness and freedom
of youth, as well as the newly attained serenity and wisdom of old

age.[1] Greek culture understood the amazingly strong power of this *senex-puer* connection, and it was a part of many of the most creative and brilliant Greek thinkers that we still respect and learn from today. Our homophobic fears do not allow us to see what was apparently very life giving for both the tutor and the student in many cases.

Some parts of us grew up too soon; some parts of us never grew up. Believe it or not, they both have something to teach us— if we can just trust and let them befriend one another a little more. One is called the old man *(senex),* and the other is called the eternal boy *(puer eternus).* We need them both. The old man *will not* change without contact with his eternal boy; the eternal boy *cannot* change without the love and challenge of his old man. Traditional religion and schooling tended to create and reward old men as does the success-oriented business world. If we only follow his lead, we become rigid and unsmiling. On the other side, postmodern culture produces a lot of eternal boys who are afraid to grow up. They are often great at art and music, humor and dance, but they don't tend to know how to support themselves or others beyond that, and actually do not have much father energy. True religion should be the harmonious integration of both. Our icon here would be the old man Simeon in the temple holding up the boy Jesus, and saying that he is now ready to die in peace (Luke 2:29–35). The old antiphon for the Divine Office on that feast put it perfectly: "The old man held the boy, but the boy held the old man." One without the other is unwhole. Let's make their complementary gifts very clear:

The Eternal Boy	The Old Man
Action that does not know	Knowledge that does not act
Fanatic	Cynic
Change	Continuity

The Young Boy and the Old Man

Elopes, expects, ready to be surprised	Holds, knows, loves, in control
Power of powerlessness (Jesus)	Powerlessness of power (the Father)
The energy of the wound	The energy to wound
Transcendent, hopeful, visionary	Immanent, grounded, remembering
Authenticity	Reality
Fun and fantasy	Work and responsibility
Inspires the blossoming of things	Knows how to gather the harvest
All space, no time (too much heaven)	All time, no space (too much earth)

The critical age is often in the forties, when the two archetypes often confront one another. Usually one is rejected forever. Because of the sophistication and success needs of our culture, most men reject the eternal boy early and become, in their worst form, heavy control freaks. Those who choose the eternal boy end up starving artists, armchair philosophers, misfits, wandering musicians or religious rebels, usually considered naïve or useless. Neither can contribute much to themselves or to society. They need their other male half.

As I look back on my own life, I'd have to say that I identified strongly with the old man even when I was fairly young. I did not participate in sports or popular music because I felt there were always things of greater consequence that I should be attending to—not realizing I was just riding my strengths and avoiding my weaknesses. When I was in the seminary, my classmates picked up on this seemingly mature side of me and I often found myself being asked for counsel and advice. But I was imbalanced, and always a bit too serious, as you probably see here. It is both my gift and my curse. But as we taught with the Enneagram, "Strangely enough, you are destroyed by your gift." Greek tragedy always understood that.

People who know me notice that I don't have any jokes to throw in when everybody's sharing jokes, and that I don't tell funny stories the way that other preachers and retreat masters do. Somehow I never learned to tell jokes and don't even do it well when I do! I love other people who are funny, and I admire them because I can't be like that. That's what the old man does: he admires in the boy what he does not have. And the boy in turn admires the old man for being what he himself is not. I don't mean to imply that I can't relax and have fun. I enjoy letting my child out as much as any man does, but in me the little boy has to ask the grandfather's permission, so to speak, and be assured that it's OK to play once in a while.

Even though because of personality or situation we might find ourselves favoring the boy or the old man in us, both are in each one of us. It is not a matter of either/or but a matter of both/and. Both the child and the grandfather have gifts to give us, and we need to appreciate both in order to enjoy our full giftedness as men. So even though I will talk about these two in terms of contrasts, we need to remember that the two are just different aspects of a balanced masculinity.

The eternal boy is hopeful and optimistic; the old man is knowledgeable and certain. To the boy, life is waiting out there to be lived; to the old man, life is the experience of having lived. Many of us cross that boundary in late middle age, when we realize that most of our life has already happened, and we find ourselves reminiscing more about the past than expecting great things in the future. The boy is full of wonder and awe, but the old man is full of recognition. If the little boy has been unduly denied, he will make a strong, almost irresistible appeal in midlife. It is a crisis of major proportions for many men in their forties, and frankly, often either gets men in trouble or actually frees them up to be human.

I can remember one time when I was traveling in a van with a group of young people from New Jerusalem. They were all from Cincinnati, and they had never been west of Indiana, but here we were together, heading for the far west. As we got to where we ought to be able to catch our first glimpse of the Rockies, they all crowded into the front of the van, waiting for the mountains to appear. Their eyes were like little children's, wondering when the mountains would appear. I remember feeling a kind of envy for those kids; I had seen the mountains so many times that I had lost the ability to be surprised or delighted by them. But I also felt something that the young people could not feel. When the mountains at last came into view, I recognized them as old friends. Distant memories returned to comfort me.

The little boy is *credulous* because he has not yet learned enough to be able to tell what's true from what isn't. In that sense, he is naïve, but his is the refreshing naïveté of the child who can listen and accept with openness. He believes what he hears because he trusts the person who is speaking to him. He follows what he is told to do because he is willing to try new things and learn from experience that he himself has not yet had. The old man, on the other hand, is the bestower of knowledge and the giver of advice that comes out of his own past experience. The old man is *credible* because he knows firsthand what he is talking about. He is believable because he lives according to what he says. He is therefore an authority because he authors new possibilities in the lives of those who listen to him, and his authorship comes not from what he has heard but from what he has lived.

The next difference has to do with what psychologists call "the shadow," by that we mean *the unseen and unacceptable side of one's personality.* The shadow self is not the bad self as such, it is just the unrecognized, repressed or denied self. It is often capable of doing bad things without knowing it, or calling them bad or evil. In other words, the shadow self is not the evil self, and in fact to struggle with it actually brings you to deep awareness. We become mature people, frankly, by our conscious relationship with our own demons and failures. But if we do not have a conscious awareness and relationship with our shadow self, it always controls us. That is the inherent narcissism of most people. That is why confession, repentance, apology, truth speaking and admission of failure are so essential to any human or spiritual or honest life. A large percentage of humanity has little self-knowledge and project most of their evil elsewhere. They never struggle with their shadow self in any real sense, but just try to think of themselves as moral and right, at all costs. Remember again Jesus' great one-liner, "Because you say, 'I see,' your guilt and blindness remain" (John 9:41). It is understandable in the young boy. It is abhorrent and sad in the old man.

Since the *puer*/boy does not know himself, he has a large shadow. He does things he does not understand, and he has motives that he is largely unaware of. The child's shadow often gets projected on to other children and adults since he does not yet understand human behavior, and he has not yet learned to look at things from other people's viewpoints. He is both critical and afraid of those around him, and he reacts unthinkingly to situations rather than responding to them out of knowledge or sympathy or clear judgments. That is exactly why children have to be taught, mentored and given example. They are not only narcissistic and largely blind, but they don't even know it yet.

The *senex*/old man, by contrast, has been around a long time and he has seen all there is to see. He understands the ways that people act and he is not thrown off by them. More importantly, he knows himself, and there is little anyone can criticize him for which he is not already aware of. He has drawn his own shadow into the light of consciousness, and so he has the psychological space to absorb the shadowy manipulations of others. And by not projecting anything on to other people, he can give them the room they need to just be themselves. He has met the primary enemy, and he knows it is himself. The boy cannot know that yet. He is not strong enough to face it. That is the job of the middle of life. And you almost always need someone to help you see or carry your shadow self, someone who loves you deeply. If not, you will never feel safe enough to face it.

Maybe I can best illustrate this with an incident that happened some years ago. I was talking with a man who had joined the community in New Jerusalem when he was still in high school and who still had a hard time with relationships. Now that puzzled me since in our own relationship, he always seemed mature. For some reason or another, he started telling me about how his friends, and especially his girlfriend, were unhappy with him. They felt he was being manipulative, and he himself felt there were aspects of his personality that grated on other people's nerves.

After listening to him for a while, I confessed to him that I had never felt him being manipulative, and I had never seen him doing the kinds of things he was accusing himself of. He looked at me wistfully and said, "Around you, my shadow never shows itself. Somehow, you have the ability to free me from my moods and fears—that whole negative side of me—and let me be the person I would really like to be." The old man has the magical power to absorb the shadow of the boy. The grandfather makes it possible for a person to leave his darkness aside and walk in the light that he knows is there but can't easily find. Actually any loving person can do that for you, in fact, that's largely what it means to be loving. You can hold for them what they cannot yet hold. You can transform for them what they cannot yet transform. You do that by not returning their negativity and fear in kind, as most people will do. When they hate or fear, you love back. That contains it and transforms the person over time. That is what God does in a consummate form and is actually what we mean by Jesus "taking away the sin of the world." He absorbs our evil, does not return it, and gradually we let go of it. He steals it from us; he takes away our sin! Good friends and true elders do the same on a much smaller scale.

Still another difference between the *puer* and the *senex* involves the way men give and receive love. A father's love, as we saw earlier, is pushing and challenging, tossing the eaglets out of the nest and telling them they can fly. The son knows he needs this, but still does not want it or appreciate it. He is not always sure where dad is coming from, and often resents this needed hardness. The young boy represents a love that comes about through being wounded, and the old man represents love that is *willing to wound*. We just call it tough love today, but men know they need it, they do respect it, even though very few seniors have the authority to know how to do it well, and very few juniors have the trust to know how to take it well. What a loss.

When I went to Japan, I was told that a young man never knows what's going to happen to him when coming to join a Zen Buddhist community. Sometimes an aspiring monk would knock on the monastery door. And sometimes he'd even have to wait two or three days before they would even let him in, to check out how badly he really wanted to be enlightened. Now, there's manly energy from day one! And the life of the novice in the monastery is just as tough. The boy is "wounded" from the beginning. Coaches and drill sergeants do much the same, but it is not spiritually tolerated in the West anymore, except among very conservative groups (who happen to be getting the most seminarians, by the way!).

A healthy and earnest young man is willing to let himself be wounded because he trusts the old man's love for him, and he believes in the goal. Countless boys let countless coaches force them to stretch to the limits of their endurance because they want what the men can call forth in them. In my own life, that place of manly testing was the seminary in the 1950s. I arrived in Cincinnati from Kansas when I was only fourteen, and I had to find my way from the train station, Union Terminal, to the Franciscan friary, about fifteen miles away, by bus. The bus delivered me to the closest stop, where there was no one there to meet me. So I trudged with my two suitcases up the mile-long road to the friary, feeling all alone and scared to death. I wonder now if that was intentional on their part.

When I was there, they got me and the other students up in the cold (and sometimes dark) early morning for prayer and meditation. The rules were strict, and our lives were pretty regimented to a degree that I sometimes resented and in ways, looking back, that were not really necessary. A young man knows and respects any system that "keeps the edges hot" for him. He knows he needs it to grow up, even though he complains all the way. One thing the old-fashioned seminary did for many of us was it made us take a good hard look at ourselves and ask what we were really there for. We weren't there for our own comfort, or any immediate payoffs, that's for sure! I suppose that other young men have had similar experiences in other places, such as the army or the football team.

Of course, the sternness of the *senex* can merely brutalize and desensitize the young man, as it often does. But the father-as-wounder, the conditional lover, also has a very special gift for the receptive son.[2] It is the polar opposite of the nurturing mother, but gives a necessary container and form and capacity for self-criticism that can be found nowhere else. It can help him face his shadow pride, control, impatience, individualism and narcissism very early in life. What a gift!

But the eternal boy is often angry with the old man for giving him the very gifts that could make him great. As a man said to me at the jail recently, "It takes us such a long time to grow up and become wise, Father, and by then we have already made all of our life's decisions and all of our mistakes." Eternal boys need old men to survive physically and psychologically. Old men need eternal boys to thrive spiritually.

Notes

1.   For a more complete description of the archetypes of the young boy and the old man, read John A. Sanford and George Lough, Ph.D., *What Men Are Like: The Psychology of Men, for Men and the Women Who Live With Them* (Mahwah, N.J.: Paulist Press, 1988), pp. 95–97.

2.   Rohr, *Adam's Return*, p. 83ff. Here I try to present the need for both conditional and unconditional love to have healthy ego structures and even healthy God structures.

TWENTY-THREE

Soul Images for Men

Four Mighty Ones are in every man. A perfect unity cannot exist but from the universal brotherhood of Eden.

—WILLIAM BLAKE, *The Four Zoas*

Since we have introduced the idea of archetypal images that form and fascinate the souls of men, I would like to offer you some images from mythology and from the collective male unconscious. There are four classic images that for some deep reason continue to appear in every age and every literature. Robert Moore, who is doing the definitive studies in this area, calls them: the king, the warrior, the magician and the lover.[1]

I have found these so helpful in recent retreat work, men's work and jail ministry that I would like to share some of what we are learning in a very condensed form. Enough I hope so that you can listen to your own journey and see if it is not true for yourself.

First, I would like to say something about archetypes. The Swiss psychologist, Carl Jung, believed that true transformation of persons happened largely, if not exclusively, through contact with images. Some of these images have an almost luminous character for us. Like meeting a god, they can both frighten and fascinate us. So much so, in fact, that they can guide and determine what we pay attention to, and often blind us to their dark sides. A young man caught up in a warrior archetype, for example, sees everything through the eyes of winning, muscles, size, power and domination.

It has little to do with logic or training, and warnings against violence will do little good. He is possessed by a "god" (or a demon, depending on how you see it). These inner "gods," or ruling images, almost totally determine whether a boy plays competitive sports, reads books, paints with pastels or tries to harmonize all of the above.

Archetypal fascinations would seem like more psycho-babble to me if I had not seen the power of stories, icons, biographies, pictures, movies, celebrities and heroes in peoples' lives. We can preach, talk and write all we want, but it is self-evident to me that *people change people.* The AIDS epidemic was largely distant and abstract for most Americans. Once Magic Johnson, the basketball player, announced that he was infected, the entire country was ablaze with fear, recognition and what some are calling the final nail in the coffin of the sexual revolution. That is the almost imperial power of a warrior and lover archetype—combined in one man. I know very few, if any, people who have been converted by theology itself. But lives of the saints, meeting the right person, great biographies and heroism can turn us around in one minute— and forever.

Archetypes are filled with generative power. They lead us into new space where we "see" ourselves for the first time. We understand our deeper desires, we know what we must do, and somehow in the fascination we even find the energy to do it. When you are in the grip of an archetype, you have vision and a deep sense of meaning for your life, even if it is just to be the best break-dancer in Brooklyn! We speak of being "possessed" by an archetype with probably the same meaning that the ancients spoke of being possessed by a devil. If you don't recognize it and somehow either respect or exorcise it, you will likely over-identify with it. It gets you and destroys you. You overdo it. The archetype must be honored for what it is, an image outside of the self that calls us to growth, change and awareness. In its negative form it can equally call us to evil, arrogance and destruction. Remember, devils were first described as merely fallen angels, and even Lucifer means the "light bearer." Just enough light to fool you.

The central masculine archetypes seem to always be about *power,* how power is good, how power is contained, how power is shared, how power is used for others, what spiritual power is and what is selfish power. What characterizes the *puer,* or the uninitiated boy, is that he is usually naïve about power. He either hates it or worships it. If he has had no proper male modeling, he hates power and uses every chance he can to show his disdain for power and authority. The irony is that he himself desires and seeks power, but just in different and disguised forms. The male *must* learn the good name for power. He must honor it, or it will almost always destroy him. Witness most of the Greek and Shakespearian tragedies.

Because we have not done our inner work, listened to our stories and initiated the younger men, power is largely out of control and universally mistrusted in western society. Our sisters are often convinced that patriarchy ("the rule of the fathers") is identical with maleness, and maleness is always about domination, war, greed and control. We have to show them and ourselves that maleness is indeed about power, but power for good, power for others, power for life and creativity. Power cannot be inherently evil. One word for the Holy Spirit in the New Testament is *dynamis,* meaning "power." All the legends and myths of history cannot be wrong. Warriors are not going to stop fascinating young boys because feminist mothers don't like it or pacifists rail against it. Like most of the great world religions, we just have to discover the meaning of the spiritual warrior.

With all that said, let us look at our four numinous male images. I say numinous intentionally because there is something about these figures, when we rightly meet them that opens us up to the Holy, the transcendent or at least our very deepest self.

The King

This image includes the Father images and carries all the connotations of authority, order, law, direction and grounding. The calm king sitting on his throne is the archetype of centeredness and security within himself. He is, therefore, a symbol of fertility and creativity for all those within his realm. To be in the king's good graces is to be OK at the core. The king in a man is secure enough to recognize, affirm and bless goodness when he sees it in others. He is not threatened by the growth or maturity of others, because he knows and loves who he himself is. You cannot threaten the king because he does not need you, or even need your admiration. He is the principle of healthy autonomy and very clear boundaries. The greater the king, the bigger the realm he can hold together. Some are kings for their own limited racial group, some hold together a "rainbow coalition," others preside over the whole domain and hold it together in unity. Thus Christians rightly speak of Jesus as "King of kings" because his universal rain "falls on the good and the bad, the just and the unjust."

The Shadow King

Each image has a clear dark side. Jesus, for example, often builds parables around evil kings and landlords. This is the image of impotence and paranoia. He is threatened by others' power and creativity, with a childish sense of his own importance. It is interesting that Saul, Herod and Pilate are usually pictured this way in movies, clearly drawing upon archetypal materials even more than the biblical text.

The shadow king disempowers and curses those outside his realm of worship. If you don't need me, I don't need you. He needs to keep subordinates inferior and in control, whether men or women. They do hold together a certain kind of realm, but it is toxic, dysfunctional and surrounded by sycophants. Hitler could hold together other fearful and hateful Germans in his realm;

certain popes can hold together card-carrying anti-communists; recent American presidents have been able to secure the kingdom of white, rich males. They undoubtedly have real king energy, but it is small and self-serving. They are the Marcoses, Battistas, Husseins and bin Ladens of recent history. They are centered and secure, but in sickness. It is repeated in the wife-beating husband and the embezzling bankers of the savings and loan scandals. All are dark kings, whose only loyalty is to their own states and security. They have great appeal to insecure people, however, because they look like they stand for something, even though it is only themselves.

The Warrior

As I mentioned earlier, it is very important that we understand the reality and power of this archetype because it is not going to go away. The warrior is dreamt about in all cultures as the image of courage, persistence, stamina and devotion to a cause. And this image is obviously much needed and very good. He maintains appropriate boundaries even at cost to himself.

Essential to the warrior is focus, clarity, absolute allegiance. This image flies in the face of all that we believe about paradox, ambiguity, civility, patience and compromise. He has no time for distinctions. Without a good king, a warrior is frankly naïve, dangerous and probably responsible for most of the aimless and almost recreational violence on this earth. The good warrior doubles his efforts when exhausted, his goal is always beyond the private ego, and he has a sense of necessary and appropriate force to achieve his purposes—no more and no less. He does not need enemies, but neither is he naïve about enemies. He is loyal to what deserves loyalty and focuses on the task without preoccupation *with* his own comfort or security. By any cultural definition that is virtue.

Because liberals have thrown out the common dark side of the warrior, they have often lost its absolutely essential gift. Now men go to karate classes, wars and armies, or fundamentalist churches with this energy because we have not learned its good meaning. Except for the medieval ideal of the knight of faith, the West has largely left this archetype uneducated. The East understands it better with the martial arts of karate, judo, aikido, the traditions of the noble samurai and the shambala warrior. This probably explains why we have been incapable of accepting the clear nonviolent teaching of Jesus. It's just not in our understanding, even though we had so many saints like Francis and Ignatius who were first of all warriors— and merely transfigured and sublimated their warrior energy.

The Black Knight/Dark Warrior

Quite simply, the dark warrior is either not in submission to a king or he is in submission to a bad king. He defines what is moral and immoral within himself, by his own egocentric criteria. He normally sees any kind of weakness or femininity as bad because it keeps him from his fanatical focus. I am personally convinced of the essential evil of militarism (on the right or on the left) because the warriors normally have to train and brutalize the young man into simplistic thinking, propaganda and a massive repression of normal human feeling. Fortunately, we have sports and games, albeit a deteriorated but safe way for warriors to act out. Unfortunately, in sports there is no real moral good or virtue to defend. For the most part, it has been dark warriors who have written history: Genghis Khan, Attila the Hun, Napoleon, Stalin, Hitler, Sadam Hussein, *and those who respond in kind to the same* (which most people don't recognize as merely more subtle dark warriors!).

The Magician

This compelling image is the archetype of awareness, consciousness, growth and transformation. He leads us to see the depth, meaning and especially the shadow side of ourselves and all things. He shows us that things are not what they seem, when looked at with "the third eye," which he helps us develop. As such, the magician or court jester is always a threat to the establishment, and it was once his job to keep the king honest and lighthearted. In the lower form the magician is a clown, a trickster or the Native American coyote. In the highest form he is the prophet or truth speaker. But the wise man's mantle covers a broad cast of characters: the father confessor, the ritual elder, the shaman, the wisdom teacher, the statesman, the spirit guide, the sorcerer, the medicine man, the mentor, the spiritual director, the liturgist and, in most cultures, the priest.

It is disappointing to me that priesthood has been made more into the king than the magician in Catholicism. In fundamentalist Protestantism, he is often a dark magician. It accounts for many of our losses and for our lack of depth and breadth. We even renamed the three magi of Matthew 2 "the three kings," even though there is no scriptural evidence for such names. The western church has consistently been more comfortable with kings than wise men. The wise men are always saying to the kings, like Nathan to David, "*You are the guilty one!*" (2 Samuel 12:7). I think religion will again gain true authority when it discovers its primary role as magician, king and lover instead of what it is now, and that is largely warrior, and immature warrior at that.

The Sorcerer's Apprentice

When a clergyman, a therapist, a guru or a faith-healer starts believing his own press, he is in trouble. When he accepts the awesome projection that people around send toward him as his own, the downward slide begins. If a spiritual or academic leader does not have a strong sense of himself as a humble instrument, if he is not himself in submission to wise direction or honest scholarship, he is perhaps the most dangerous of all the archetypes. He becomes a charlatan, an Elmer Gantry, a televangelist, a pseudo scholar, a snake charmer, a crowd pleaser, a president quoting Scripture for purposes of reelection.

How does one handle the mantle of spiritual or intellectual power? Frankly, most people don't do it very well. It is too inflating and associates you with the gods. To "traffic in holy things" was once called the egregious sin of simony, and it is always the great temptation of the professionally religious person. I have great sympathy for the major religious figures that have fallen in recent years. If you do not have a strong tradition of spiritual direction, then illusion and infantile grandiosity are almost inevitable in this area. When we wear special clothes, we are asking for this projection. We can use it well to heal, to forgive, to proclaim, to celebrate the holy mysteries. But we can also use it too easily to avoid our inner substance. Intellectuals often do the same under the mantle of education and mental superiority and various images of academic tenure. University faculties can be filled with huge egos, pettiness and a preference for information over transformation.

The Lover

When we are captured by the archetype of the lover, we know how to delight, to appreciate, to enjoy that which is good, true and beautiful. We see the color, form, texture and ultimate gratuity of things. In its highest state, therefore, it is the contemplative who can value things in themselves and for themselves and see the hidden beauty of "deep down things." It is also the poet, the artist, the musician, the romantic, those who know how to sip the divine nectar in all events and relationships.

Without the lover, life is frankly boring and eventually sour. The lover does not apologize for pleasure or joy. He is the fertility god in every man, always ready to dance and display. In mythology he is Dionysius, in literature perhaps Zorba the Greek, and in

Christianity he is the fiery Holy Spirit who blows where he wills.

Unfortunately, the archetype of the lover has always been a bit wild and scary for the rational western church. He fell into the unconscious, but periodically shows himself in movements like the Renaissance, the worship of the Madonna (fertility was more safely contained and valued in the feminine), elaborate liturgies, saints like Francis of Assisi, Philip Neri and John XXIII, plus the predictable pendulum swings like the hippie generation and the sexual revolution. The lover will not be denied his entrance. If the king holds the real together in unity, if the warrior protects the necessary boundaries of the real, if the magician shows us how to live the paradox, depth, and dark side of things, then the lover holds it all together with the sweet glue of appreciation and occasional ecstasy.

The Addict

When the lover can no longer enjoy, he will create instant and artificial enjoyment. When the lover is not allowed, he goes underground and finds secret and often destructive pleasures. When the lover is rejected, he retreats into negativity, cynicism and self-destruction. Without the sweetness of the lover, life is frankly not worth living. The usual substitute is to resort to addictive patterns. Patterns of order, patterns of cold duty, patterns of seeming control, patterns of thinking (obsessive), patterns of feeling (hysterical), patterns of hoarding and protecting (paranoid) and patterns of instant gratification like drinking, drugs, buying, promiscuity and overeating. He moves toward narcissism, caring for himself because he does not feel cared for by life itself.

It is clear that our culture largely falls into this category. We are would-be and wounded lovers. We were somehow given promises that did not come to pass, and we lack the cultural discipline and containers to hold us back from the long slide downward. Programs for addictions will continue to grow in numbers and in need. They have named the shape of sin better than the contemporary churches, who still do not see the connection between their repression of the positive lover archetype and the widespread emergence of the addict.[2] If we had a more positive and integrated attitude toward pleasure, sexuality and embodiment, we would probably not have the destructive over-reaction we see today. The rejected god normally returns as a demon.

These different faces of the masculine attract us at the different times of our life. There is no correct pattern or superior archetype, in my opinion. The important thing is that we honor all of them and each of them when they show themselves in our friendships and fascinations. There will normally be one that we are already strongly identified with, and usually one or the other that we mistrust or even deny. He often holds the secret to our wholeness. David, for example, was clearly king, warrior and lover, but until he receives the challenge of the prophet/magician Nathan, he is still unwhole and even dangerous to himself and others. Only with Nathan's critique does David become the archetypal Jewish whole man.

The important thing is that we stay on the path and let the four parts of our soul mutually regulate and balance one another. If you over-identify with one for too long, you will normally move toward the dark side. In other words, if you are only a king, unbalanced by warrior, lover and magician, you will soon be a bad king. If you are only a lover, with no sense of king or warrior boundaries, you will soon be an addict. If you are only a warrior, without the nuancing of the magician, or a good leader, you will probably end up a terrorist or a fanatic.

If you fear that this is a new game of "dungeons and dragons," as one super-Christian accused it of being, I encourage you to examine the ancient and traditional baptismal rite of the church. Right after the holy dunking, the priest anoints you with scented oil (the lover) and encourages you to follow Christ as "priest (magician), prophet (warrior) and king." We always knew this, but just did not know that we knew it.

Notes

1. Robert Moore and D. Gillette, *King Warrior Magician Lover* (San Francisco: HarperSanFrancisco, 1990).

2. Richard Rohr, "How Do We Breathe Under Water?" Recorded conference, 2005 (Center for Action and Contemplation, Box 12464, Albuquerque, NM 87195).

TWENTY-FOUR

The Ancient Language of Spirituality

Teach us to care and not to care,
Teach us to sit still even among these rocks,
Our peace in His will,
And even among these rocks.

—T.S. ELIOT, "Ash Wednesday"

The language of the first half of the male life journey is the language of *ascent,* the earnest and necessary idealism that characterizes all healthy young men. It is a heroic language of winning, succeeding, triumphing over ego and obstacles. Without such vision and effort, men remain cowering in a small and powerless world. The man has to climb in the beginning, or he cannot test his metal, find his best self, say no to his false self or triumph over egocentricity.

But this same task of ascent becomes dangerous in the second half of a man's life.[1] It becomes disguised egocentricity, climbing at all costs, misusing power, using ideology and principles to avoid relationship—what Saint Paul calls law instead of Spirit in his letter to the Galatians. Thus we see that all great spiritual teachers, like Jesus himself, seem to have two sets of teachings: one for the early multitudes and another for the mature disciples (e.g., Matthew 13:10–12; 1 Corinthians 3:1–3; Hebrews 5:12–14).

Much spiritual damage has been done in failing to make this distinction. Institutional religion and most religious movements prefer to keep their members at the early stage. They can be managed better, it holds the group together, it feels like "real" morality, but they sacrifice depth, initiative and creativity. It is merely the necessary journey of self control, but knows nothing of giving up control—which is the real spiritual issue. It is the perennial problem of both the military and of religion. The false king wants order and predictability, not creativity or maturity. Organizationally he is right, of course. Spiritually, however, he is dead wrong.

No wonder that almost all primal cultures see the need for male initiation rites, mentors and elders to prepare people ahead of time for transitioning to the second half of life. Someone has to oversee the first stage journey and also teach them that *it is only the first stage.* No wonder that they set out to actually "wound" the boy early. He had to be prepared for the falling apart of his game. He had to be taught how to descend from his tower. He had to deal with the inevitability of failure. He had to learn how to turn his wound into a sacred wound. Without such "ways of the cross" we will continue to have more "religion-as-self-advancement" instead of any real transformation of persons into God. I have no doubt this is the basis of disillusionment with western institutional religion. People no longer trust new belief systems that merely surround old egos.

The great spiritual teachers have a different wisdom for the second half of the journey. It is no longer an "ego morality" of world clarifying dualisms. It is no longer concerned with mere boundaries and identity. It is no longer concerned with questions of "Who am I?" or "Who is in and who is out?" It is no longer concerned with creating a proper self, "a grain of wheat," but true spiritual teachers are concerned, like Jesus, with teaching the grain of wheat to "die" or they know it will remain "just a grain of wheat" and not bear "a rich harvest" (John 12:24). That is always the difficult task of mature religion, and no one fights it more, like the disciples themselves (see Mark 8:31—10:45), than *men,* and religious men in particular, who have built themselves a superior and comfortable self-image.

Hopefully by the second half of life, men have met the God who "makes his sun rise on the bad and the good, and causes rain to fall on the just and the unjust" (Matthew 5:45b). Hopefully their self-serving, black-and-white worldview has fallen apart for them, by reason of failure, suffering and sin. The language changes from a language of ascending, achieving and attaining to a humble language of *descent.* We Catholics called it the way of the cross and visualized it in all our churches as the Stations of the Cross. Franciscans call it poverty, Carmelites call it nothingness, Buddhists call it emptiness, and Judaism calls it the desert. We kept all these metaphors, but in cultures of progress, like ours, we lost the essential message. It was just too countercultural. It felt like going backward and down.

For a mature man in the second half of life, heroism is no longer the goal or concern. Now the goal is something that we can no longer manufacture, control or even possess as our own: holiness. Holiness is given and received; it is utterly but quietly transforming; sometimes it even feels and looks like "sinfulness" to the uninitiated. Holiness seldom looks heroic until the holy ones have been buried for a few centuries, and we can safely begin the canonization process. Holiness has to do with who we are in God, where we abide as a "self" with an utterly reconstituted sense of our own personhood. Gabriel Marcel calls it "the subordination of the self to a Deeper Reality that is more deeply me than I am by myself." Holiness has to do with *being* in God, whereas the early heroic journey has more to do with *doing* and achieving a self.

Saint Paul describes his conversion in at least two stages. The first is the dramatic encounter on the Damascus road. The second he describes more subtly and humbly in the third chapter of his letter to the Philippians. Unsurprisingly, it is now twenty years later, and he is powerlessly chained in prison. Listen to these amazing words: "...[I]n righteousness based on the law I was blameless. [But] whatever gains I had, these I have come to consider a loss because of Christ.... I consider them so much rubbish, that I may gain Christ and be found in him..." (3:6b–7, 8b–9a). The Law that got him off to a good start ("advantage") is now actually a liability. (If you have any doubt about Paul's strong feelings here, the word translated as "rubbish" is the four-letter word we use for excrement.) This is altogether amazing, considering Paul's heroic and youthful love for the Law, a love that led him to murder Christians. Paul was an earnest believer, which is often a good place to start, it seems, despite its common excesses.

We see the same pattern in John the Baptist. He neither ate nor drank (see Matthew 11:18); he lived ascetically in the desert, wearing coarse clothing; he had hard words for almost everybody. God uses such energy and absolutism to get young men started on the spiritual journey: "Amen, I say to you, among those born of woman there has been none greater than John the Baptist, yet the least in the kingdom of God is greater than he" (Matthew 11:11).

The journey that Jesus walks has a lot more patience and compassion than John or Paul's early strident voices. Yet God was able to use both of them well, precisely because they had done the first half of life issues with such passion, self-sacrifice and conviction. The important thing is the sequencing and the transition, which I think is uniquely the work of the Spirit. You cannot maneuver it by logic, persuasion or Bible quoting. No wonder that the Catholic tradition put so much emphasis on the importance of father confessors and spiritual directors. Book answers are not sufficient in the crucial times of transition. The rules that help us in stage one might just be toxic in later stages; we will need humility—maybe even authority—to let go of that which seemed to save us earlier.

The Ancient Language of Spirituality

In Robertson Davies' *Deptford Trilogy,* the old priest says what only old age can allow us to say. He observes that church teaching, rather than reflect the certainty and strength of youth, needs to take into account the experiences of a lifetime and the uncertainty that comes with age. Then perhaps we can make sense of life and maybe make it bearable.

The young man with a "blessed rage for order" solves his own ego problem, but leaves too many victims in his wake: the weak, the outsider, women, the homosexual, the non-Christian, the foreigner, the sinner whom he perhaps condescends to love "while still hating the sin." He can maintain his saved and superior self image, while actually remaining quite unloving, untouched and self-sufficient. It takes mellow old grandfathers to teach the young turks the way of compassion and the way of patience. No wonder most cultures look to seniors and "senates" for leadership. Yet the author Robert Moore rightly says that you seldom access "king energy" much before fifty years of age.

The language of descent is either learned by midlife (normally through suffering and the experience of powerlessness), or we inevitably move into a long day's journey of accusing, resentment and negativity, circling our wagons as the hurts and disappointments of life gather around us: "I am right and others are wrong. I have a right to my judgments and I will continue to use valuable energy to justify them." I have visited too many old men and retired priests in nursing homes to doubt this common pattern. When midlife no longer allowed them to ascend or to deny their dark side, far too many men either shut down or kept running. The price is a world of men who do not age well, who are emotionally, spiritually, intellectually unavailable—or just eccentric. These are the dads, priests and leaders that we all laugh about but seldom take seriously.

I want to present a diagram (on pages 166 and 167) that I use on men's retreats in different countries for those who learn better through visualization. I hope it will give you a pictorial sense of the stages of ascent and descent. Know, however, that life is never a straight line, but much more a spiral. We perhaps go through these cycles of death and resurrection many times, but hopefully on a new level after each learning curve.

I hope this diagram helps us to see that what is good and necessary for the young man is often deadening for the older man. Black-and-white worldviews, heroic willfulness, get the young man started and rightly directed so he will one day be secure enough and strong enough to understand the true meaning of the cross.

If we try to give the young man the full doctrine of "the cross," it will either go over his head, he will see it as a mere Christian logo, or he will create artificial "crosses" (paralysis, analysis, neurosis) to advance his spiritual ego. It is no surprise that Jesus himself did not talk about the cross or carry his own until at least the age of thirty. Young men (and often severely humiliated men) will turn every spiritual teaching, the church, the sacraments and even the gospel into another way to ascend and feel superior. Maybe that is why Jesus taught mature men, not children or youth. The "rich and young man" (Mark 10:17–22) will always turn the message of discipleship into another form of personal advancement. We forget that even the concern to "go to heaven" is initially little more than disguised self-interest. "What must I do to inherit eternal life?" the rich young man asks. Jesus not only does not really answer his question (because it is the wrong question), but he just tells him to "descend" from his power position, "go away and get rid of all your possessions." Money is only the metaphor here; the real possession he has to get rid of is his ego. But he is the only personally invited would-be disciple who ever walks away from Jesus. He is too young and too comfortable.

Let me end with a quote from Carl Jung, in his *Collected Works* (8, 784): "We cannot live the afternoon of life according to the program of life's morning; for what was great in the morning will be of little importance in the evening, and what in the morning was true will at evening have become a lie."

Note

1.   D'Arcy and Rohr, *Spirituality for the Two Halves of Life*.

THE MALE SPIRITUAL JOURNEY

STAGE OF ASCENT
Needs to *make* and *keep* promises to grow

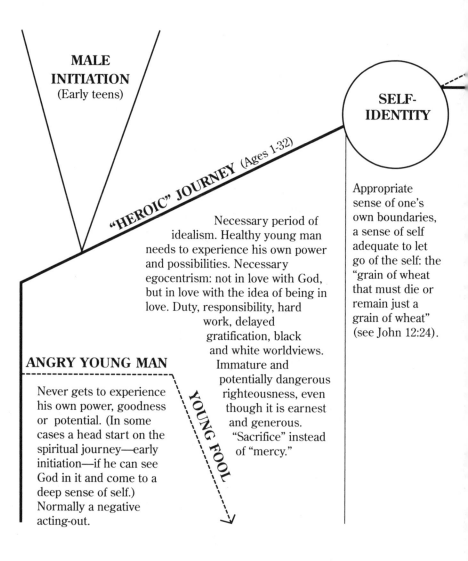

MALE INITIATION
(Early teens)

SELF-IDENTITY

"HEROIC" JOURNEY (Ages 1-32)

Necessary period of idealism. Healthy young man needs to experience his own power and possibilities. Necessary egocentrism: not in love with God, but in love with the idea of being in love. Duty, responsibility, hard work, delayed gratification, black and white worldviews. Immature and potentially dangerous righteousness, even though it is earnest and generous. "Sacrifice" instead of "mercy."

Appropriate sense of one's own boundaries, a sense of self adequate to let go of the self: the "grain of wheat that must die or remain just a grain of wheat" (see John 12:24).

ANGRY YOUNG MAN

Never gets to experience his own power, goodness or potential. (In some cases a head start on the spiritual journey—early initiation—if he can see God in it and come to a deep sense of self.) Normally a negative acting-out.

YOUNG FOOL

STAGE OF DESCENT
Needs to rest in God's promises and model the wholeness/holiness for other

OLD FOOL ···→ Doesn't get it; tries to keep ascending despite the evidence and the invitation; the shallow male.

CRISIS OF LIMITATION
(Ages 35-50)

EMBITTERING JOURNEY ---→

WISDOM JOURNEY

Confrontation, but no enlightenment. Wounds did not become "sacred" wounds; still looking for something to blame. The negative and cynical man.

HOLY FOOL →

The mid-life crisis: a time of inner loss of meaning, sometimes accompanied by failure, falling apart and "acting out" to regain power and control. Confrontation with one's limits, with paradox and mystery—with the cross. Heroic virtues don't usually work anymore, nor do they always help. Needs humility, honesty. Early movement from self-control to the beginnings of God control.

Needs spiritual guidance because rules no longer work in their old form. Letting go, trust, patience, surrender, holy abandonment, compassion, the dark night of faith; the Abrahamic Journey from what you have to what you don't have. Finally secure enough to be insecure. Time of painful insights and major surgery. Painfully redefining victory and success; putting on the mind of Christ, the Paschal Mystery. Cannot fake prayer anymore, but must pray to survive. The shadow is not just tolerated, but embraced, forgiven and seen as gift. The rejected stone becomes the cornerstone (see 1 Peter 2:7). "Mercy" instead of "sacrifice."

God's beloved son, the mellow "grandfather" who can hold together the paradoxes because God has done it in him. God is finally in control. Return to simplicity, to the garden; beyond judgments, "reason" and control to wisdom. Being human more important than self-image, role, power, prestige or possessions. He has it all!

TWENTY-FIVE

The Grand Father

You may be 38 years old, as I happen to be. And one day, some great opportunity stands before you and calls you to stand up for some great principle, some great issue, some great cause. And you refuse to do it because you are afraid.... You refuse to do it because you want to live longer.... You're afraid that you will lose your job, or you are afraid that you will be criticized or that you will lose your popularity, or you're afraid that somebody will stab you, or shoot at you or bomb your house; so you refuse to take the stand. Well you may go on and live until you are 90, but you're just as dead at 38 as you would be at 90. And the cessation of breathing in your life is but the belated announcement of an earlier death of the spirit.

—MARTIN LUTHER KING, JR.[1]

The final stage of the wisdom journey is symbolized by the ruling image of the king, the holy fool, the old wizard, the saint or what I just like to call the grand father. I began with this compelling quote from Martin Luther King because I want to point out that sometimes younger men can already carry such greatness and largeness of spirit. I am not talking about old grandpas as much as "grand" fathers, *men who hold, carry, purify and transform life in grand ways.* Martin Luther King was named well because he was already an archetypal "king" at the age of thirty-eight! When you can even love your enemies, you are surely a king, and Martin Luther King made an art form of loving his enemies.

I myself was blessed with a grand father in the person of my own dad—which is why, perhaps, I identified more with the archetype of the old man more than the boy even when I was young. My father was (he died in 1999 at age eighty-nine) a simple man, not highly educated, but very wise. He had the wisdom to know what he knew and to know what he did not know. He had the wisdom to trust that what he did not understand might still be good, even if he did not understand it. He had a natural respect for the goodness of others. And he could encourage others to trust in themselves and to go their own way, even if their way was not his way. Because of his ability to trust and encourage me even when he did not understand where God was calling me, I was able to become a priest and venture into a personal vocation that was very different from his. He did not need me to mirror him. He was able to mirror me. That is the healthy freedom and generativity of a mature man.

Even when I was an adolescent, my father grandly trusted and affirmed me. When I wanted to go out, he never demanded that I explain where I was going. He simply trusted me, and through his trust I learned responsibility. When I left so young to go to the seminary, he backed me up every step of my fourteen years away from home. After I became a public speaker, he and my mother would sometimes come and listen to a talk that I was giving, and I still felt that same trust, and even admiration, coming from him. He did not usually understand, I'm sure, everything I was saying. It was not his field of interest. He was a farmer and a mechanic and a painter for the Atchison, Topeka and Santa Fe. I can still see him sitting in the front row and trusting that whatever I am saying has to be good, just because I'm saying it. In this he was probably like most fathers. His respect for me enabled me to be the man that I am and to say what I have to say still today.

When we can trust others like that—when we can trust God and trust life even when we do not fully understand—we too can be grand fathers. When we can let go of our need for everything to be as we want it, and our own need to succeed, we can then encourage the independent journey and the success of others. When we can let go of our fear of failure and our fear of pain, we are free to trust life just as it comes. We are able to affirm that, if God allows it, there must be something OK about it. That sounds like passivity or fatalism, but that is not what I mean at all. There is a letting go that is passivity, but there is a letting go that is egolessness, trust and surrender. The first is dangerous; the second is sanctity. The grand father is able to relinquish center stage and to stand on the sidelines, and thus be in solidarity with those who need his support.

The strongest image of that in the Bible is probably, however, a woman. It is Mary standing at the foot of the cross (John 19:25). Note it says "standing," that is, with dignity, holding the pain strongly until it is transformed. She is not hysterical, not prostrate, not accusing, not blaming, not even trying to take him down, or save his reputation—or hers. She is the clear feminine side of what we are talking about, the grand "mother" archetype.

Grand father or grand mother energy is an energy that is quiet and secure. It has been tested and not found wanting. It does not need to prove itself any longer, and so it can approve and bless the efforts of others who are not yet sure of themselves. Children can feel secure in the presence of their grandparents because, while mom and dad are still rushing to find their way through life's journey, grandpa and grandma have hopefully become spacious. They can contain problems, inconsistencies, inconveniences and contradictions—after a lifetime of practicing and learning.

Grand fathers can deeply trust life precisely because they have come to terms with death. They know that pain is not the enemy, but that fear of pain is. They have lived through enough of life to understand that in the long run, life is stronger than death. Life has a vitality that may be temporarily slowed down, but inevitably life energy will overcome the destructive forces of death. We see this principle at work on the large scale in many underdeveloped countries, where despite years of oppression people can still be hopeful and even happy. We see it also at work in other groups who are working to improve their situations, and where individuals overcome great odds, fighting against poverty, addiction and disease, to lead fulfilling and rewarding lives.

Grand fathers recognize the surge of the divine spirit in the human situation. Because they can trust that ultimately God is in control, they can let go of their own desire to control reality and to bend others to their will. They can stop trying to force life, as they often did when they were younger men, and simply allow it to flow in the patterns that eventually—if not immediately and directly—lead to greater life.

This is not to say that grand fathers are naïve. They have seen enough of death that they know what it looks like, even when it comes under the guise of false promises and clever rationalizations. But they can look beyond the ignorance of the young who desire money and success, power and pleasure, with the wisdom of knowing that in the long run these are transitory illusions. They have heard enough of politicians' promises and advertisers' claims to realize that these are largely empty, but they are not disturbed by the hollowness of talk because, in truth, they have begun to inhabit the next world. They have already begun to pass over. They have died many times, and they know that the next death will not harm them. "What have I ever lost by dying?" they say.

Younger men need to fight against the forces of death in their own lives and in the life of their society—and rightly so, for their calling is to assume responsibility for the direction of life and to courageously work for their own good and the good of others. Grand fathers, however, understand that every human decision inevitably mixes good and bad, and that every social situation is a mixture of light and darkness. The courage of the grand father, therefore, is not to fight death but to *affirm a life that is bigger than death.* They recognize that, as Jesus said, "No one is good but God alone" (Mark 10:18b), so they are free of the illusion that any other good is completely good or that even bad people are totally bad. They are beyond hating, and also beyond idolizing.

They now know that the first half of life was as necessary as the second. To pretend to jump to the second half of life before fighting, needing, cursing and failing is often a lazy and dishonest posture. I see this in much fundamentalist religion and simplistic politics. Almost an infallible sign that someone is at an enlightened stage of life is that they can have patience and understanding with people who are still fighting, needing too much, cursing and failing!

Grand fathers can trust life because they have seen more of it than younger men have, and they can trust death because they are closer to it than younger men are. Something has told them along the way that who they are now is never the final stage, and this one isn't either. You need to be close enough to your own death to see it coming and recognize that death and life are united in an eternal embrace, and one is not the end of the other. Death is what it is. Death is not easy, but it is a part of life, and they know that life is good. The body is a lesson; once we have learned the lesson, we can let go of it. You are a grand father when you are ready to let go. To the grand father, death is no longer an enemy, but as Saint Francis called it, a "welcome sister."

The soul of the grand father is large enough to embrace the death of the ego and to affirm the life of God in itself and others, despite all imperfections. Its spaciousness accepts all the opposites in life—masculine and feminine, unity and difference, victory and defeat, us and them and so on—because it has accepted the opposition of death itself. The grand father no longer needs the luxury of utterly clear principles to assure him of each decision. If he has walked the hero's journey, he knows that his beliefs have less to do with unarguable conclusions than scary encounters with life and the living God. He has come to realize that spiritual growth is not so much learning, as it is unlearning, a radical openness to the truth no matter what the consequences or where it leads. He understands that he does not so much grasp the truth as let go of his ego—personal obstacles to truth.

He has learned that it is indeed "honesty that will set you free" (John 8:32) much more than mere theoretical truth. He now sees that judgmentalism and righteousness is not so much seeking truth as it is seeking control. He has learned that conversion is a process of listening ever more deeply to the other—and to the Other. Religion has become naked presence more than explanations.

Perhaps more than anything else, one becomes a grand father in learning to deal with limits graciously. *The joyful acceptance of a limited world, of which I am only a small moment and limited part*—this is probably the clearest indication of a man in his fullness. What he once fought for—perfect freedom—he now finds in the even imperfect events and institutions of this world. Witness a Saint Paul, a Dietrich Bonhoeffer or a Nelson Mandela in prison. The grand father largely mistrusts the world's definition of freedom. Like Aristotle, he understands that freedom only comes alive in a person already committed to virtue and freedom from oneself is the only real freedom.

The chaos and pluralism of our times will probably continue to push many men toward taking refuge behind false boundaries, such as patriarchy, nationalism, racism, fundamentalism and sexism, instead of remaining on the labyrinthine journey called faith. Others will continue to move toward psycho-babble and New Age shapelessness precisely in order to avoid all boundaries and surrenders. I cannot imagine a true grand father who is not a contemplative in some form. And a contemplative is one *who lives and returns to the center within himself, and yet he knows that the Center is not himself. He is only a part, but a gracious and grateful part at that.*

Maybe we need to stop describing this in terms of concepts and just name a few grand fathers whom we all might know. We need their power in our times, and only their lives and witness can pass it on to us. I know you could add many more, and I hope you do, but these are some who occur to me: Abraham Lincoln, Albert Schweitzer, Dag Hammarskold, U Thant, John XXIII, Dietrich Bonhoeffer, Mikhail Gorbachev, Jean Vanier, Thich Nhat Hanh, Martin Luther King, Jr., Mohandas Gandhi, Martin Buber, Anwar Sadat, Abraham Heschel, Thomas Merton, Dom Helder Camara, Thomas Dooley, Hubert Humphrey, John Howard Griffin, Jimmy Carter, Cardinal Bernardin, Julius Nyrere and Nelson Mandela.

Needless to say, we are not mass-producing elders in American society today, for it takes a wise man to call forth a wild man to produce another wise man. It sometimes feels to me as though we are waiting for a global act of spiritual spontaneous combustion. But since God has been humble and patient enough to wait and keep trying, I guess we can too.

Note

1. D'Arcy and Rohr, *Spirituality for the Two Halves of Life.* Another tape set called "Adult Christianity: And How to Get There" was also done by Richard Rohr and Father Ron Rolheiser, o.m.i., and is available from the Center for Action and Contemplation. It probably depends on whether you want a male and female read on the issue or two theologians talking about it.

Appendix

A Structure for Your Men's Group

The Number 30

We have decided to make 30 our symbolic M.A.L.Es (Men as Learners and Elders) number.

It is the symbolic age when men begin to ask adult questions of themselves and clearly leave "youth."

It is the age when Jesus seems to have "made his statement" about life and death.

On the 30th of each month we will join in a conscious prayer day for other men and solidarity day with other men around the world.

On the 30th of the month we will examine what we have done for our brothers, fathers, sons and other men in the previous month, and maybe what we could do in the month ahead.

And we suggest that 30-30-30 might even be a good structure for starting a men's group:

30-30-30 Meetings

★ Ideal size might be about six men for a 90-minute meeting.

★ Official time is held to, so men know what they can expect and have committed to.

★ If men want to go longer, the whole group can decide, or excuse those who have to go with no pressure or explanations needed.

★ 30-30-30 minute meetings would be an ideal time frame that men can commit to:

> BACKGROUND Time: 30 minutes of sharing "where I am right now."

> MIDGROUND Time: 30 minutes of sharing on the selected theme for the meeting.

> FOREGROUND Time: 30 minutes of what I need to do/change/improve in the month ahead.

I would not hold rigidly to these three categories in terms of time, but they do allow men to know what to possibly expect, which takes away some natural resistance to meetings.

I would suggest that you begin and end meetings with a short prayer, composed spontaneously by a different man each time.

M.A.L.Es.

Men As Learners and Elders

www.malespirituality.org

menswork@cacradicalgrace.org

VISION

We reclaim the spiritual initiation of men through experiential journeying into the True Self, creating a tradition for future generations.

MISSION *We commit to:*

★ Directing men in lifelong spiritual learning

★ Training men to be Elders

★ Maintaining ongoing relationships with participants

★ Providing Men's Rites of Passage

★ Developing additional Rites as needed

PHILOSOPHY *We believe:*

★ Every man is a Beloved Son of God.

★ Men are ready for serious spiritual journeys.

★ Our message is grounded in the Christian Paschal Mystery while integrating the symbols and rituals from other religions and cultures.

★ Men must seek to improve their conscious contact with God through prayer and meditation.

★ Men must have the affirmation and guidance of wise mentors.

★ Men have a need and responsibility to mentor future generations.

★ In a universal message that transcends the boundaries of race, nation, culture, gender, economics/class, politics, sexual orientation and religious differences.

★ Men must seek honest mutuality in their relationships with women in thought, word and deed.

★ Men must recognize and critique their own power in regard to women, minorities and the poor, and use their power for justice in the world.

★ There is a need for collaborating with like-minded groups and other faith traditions.

Men **A**s **L**earners and **E**lders is a program of the
Center for Action and Contemplation, Albuquerque, NM
www.cacradicalgrace.org

Other works by Richard Rohr, O.F.M.
Available from St. Anthony Messenger Press

Books

The Great Themes of Scripture: New Testament with Joseph Martos

The Great Themes of Scripture: Old Testament with Joseph Martos

Hope Against Darkness: The Transforming Vision of Saint Francis in an Age of Anxiety

Jesus' Plan for a New World: The Sermon on the Mount with John Feister

Radical Grace: Daily Meditations with John Feister

Why Be Catholic? Understanding Our Experience and Tradition with Joseph Martos

CDs and Cassettes

Authentic Religion: Membership or Transformation?

Breathing Under Water: Spirituality and the Twelve Steps

Catholicism: More Than a 'Head Trip'

Dying: You Need it For Life

Faith: Recovering the Language of Belief

Faith in Exile: Biblical Spirituality for Our Time

Fire From Heaven: A Retreat for Men

Gravity and Grace: Insights Into Christian Ministry

Great Themes of Paul: Life as Participation

Healing Our Violence through the Journey of Centering Prayer with Thomas Keating, O.C.S.O.

Hearing the Wisdom of Jesus

Jesus: Forgiving Victim, Transforming Savior

Letting Go: A Spirituality of Subtraction

Life-Changing Teachings of Richard Rohr, O.F.M.: An Introductory Set

'Love Your Enemy': The Gospel Call to Nonviolence

A Man's Approach to God: Four Talks on Male Spirituality

The Maternal Face of God

Men and Women: The Journey of Spiritual Transformation

New Great Themes of Scripture

The Parables: Letting Jesus Teach Us

Preparing for Christmas With Richard Rohr

The Quest for Holy Wisdom

Rebuild the Church: Richard Rohr's Challenge for the New Millennium

Sermon on the Mount

A Spirituality for the Two Halves of Life with Paula D'Arcy

The Spirituality of Imperfection

True Self / False Self